Seferis
AND FRIENDS

OTHER BOOKS BY GEORGE THANIEL

Homage to Byzantium: The Life and Work of Nikos Gabriel Pentzikis (1983)
The Lepidopterist of Suffering, Nikos Kachtitsis (1981)
The Nails (1968; second edition 1981)

Seferis
AND FRIENDS

(Some of George Seferis' Friends in the English-Speaking World)

by George Thaniel

Edited by Ed Phinney

THE MERCURY PRESS

Copyright © Edward Phinney and George Stubos for the Estate of George Thaniel, 1994

ALL RIGHTS RESERVED.
No part of this book may be reproduced by any means without the written permission of the publisher, with the exception of brief passages for review purposes. Any request for photocopying or other reprographic copying must be sent in writing to the Canadian Reprography Collective, 379 Adelaide Street West, Suite M1, Toronto, Ontario, Canada, M5V 1S5.
§
The publisher gratefully acknowledges the financial assistance of the Canada Council, the Ontario Arts Council, and the Ontario Publishing Centre, in its ongoing publishing program, and the Canadian Federation for the Humanities in the publication of this book.
   The publisher particularly wishes to thank Ed Phinney for his help.

Cover design by TASK
Composed in Bembo
Printed and bound in Canada by Metropole Litho
Printed on acid-free paper

First Printing, February, 1994
1 2 3 4 5   98 97 96 95 94

CANADIAN CATALOGUING IN PUBLICATION

Thaniel, George, 1938-1991
Seferis and friends
Includes bibliographical references.
ISBN 1-55128-008-6
1. Seferis, George, 1900-1971 - Biography.
2. Seferis, George, 1900-1971 - Correspondence.
3. Poets, Greek (Modern) - Biography.
I. Title.
PA5610.S36Z83 1994   889'.132   C94-930349-6

Represented in Canada by the Literary Press Group
Distributed in Canada by General Publishing
and in the United States by Inland Book Company (selected titles)

The Mercury Press
137 Birmingham Street
Stratford, Ontario
Canada N5A 2T1

For Nick and Debbie Ruscillo, Nephew and Niece

Author's Preface & Acknowledgements

Contrary to the fate of other writers who, once they die, go into an eclipse, George Seferis has continued to interest critics and readers since his death in 1971. In Greece there has been an impressive output of books and articles on the work of Seferis. The publications in English make a respectable but still limited total. Only a small selection of Seferis' essays is available in English, and only one of his personal diaries has been translated *in toto*— otherwise, we have excerpts in translation included in articles. On the critical front, apart from the pioneering work on Seferis by Edmund Keeley and Philip Sherrard, one may cite the books by Rachel Hadas and Carmen Capri-Karka, some perceptive articles and reviews by Roderick Beaton, the informative papers by John Rexine, and several articles by the Greek scholars George Savidis and Nasos Vayenas (whose work is mostly in Greek). There is certainly room for more, and the present book is meant as a helpful contribution.

Most of the material in this book was researched at the Gennadeios Library, and written during the writer's sabbatical year (1985-1986), in Athens, Greece, with the help of a fellowship gratefully received from the Social Sciences and Humanities Research Council of Canada. My thanks go, first of all, to Mrs. Maro Seferis, who allowed the research at the Gennadeios and also at her home, where much of Seferis' correspondence and other biographical material still remains, and then to the staff of the Gennadeios who assisted me in my work there. Mrs. Seferis discussed George Seferis with me several times as well, and has kindly permitted me to edit and publish a number of the English letters that Seferis had received or to use such letters in my discussion. Several colleagues and friends have read parts of the book and contributed comments. Dr. E.S. Phinney of the Department of Classics, University of Massachusetts at Amherst, has read most of the book and advised me on points of style. Sir Steven Runciman and Professor A.R. Burn, two of Seferis' surviving English friends, as well as the recently deceased John Lehmann, kindly corresponded with me on Seferis.

Earlier versions of the first three chapters have appeared in the journals *Modern Greek Studies Yearbook*, 2 (1986); *Journal of Modern Greek Studies*, 5,1 (1987); and *Scripta Mediterranea*, VIII-IX (1987-1988). Pending permission, I am quoting Seferis' poetry in English from the Keeley-Sherrard expanded (1981) edition published by Princeton University Press. Faber and Faber Ltd. has allowed me to quote poems by Lawrence Durrell from Durrell's *Collected Poems: 1931-1974*. All translations from Seferis' prose works, unless indicated otherwise, are my own.

George Thaniel

Editor's Preface

"Syrup for the cake
once each year
tribute for the dead."
— George Thaniel (tr. E. Phinney)

Professor George Thaniel died of sudden kidney failure in Athens, Greece, on June 21, 1991. (I have described his successful career as a scholar and poet in *The Modern Greek Studies Yearbook*, Volume 8, 395-407.) At the time of his death, he had completed a rough draft of this book— a book that fulfilled his life-long ambition to write a monograph about George Seferis and Seferis' connections with the English-speaking authors T.S. Eliot, Lawrence Durrell, and Henry Miller, among others. Thaniel conducted much of the research in Athens at the home of George Seferis' widow, Maro Seferis, and in the Gennadeios Library. He came back each evening, I remember, to his Athens apartment and typed his transcriptions of and reactions to the copies of letters by George Seferis or sent by others to Seferis. A number of these letters were nearly illegible copies, and I helped him decipher many mysterious scrawls.

George Thaniel was extremely interested in the great Greek poet Seferis and his interactions with English-speaking authors. This subject represented for him an opportunity to commemorate his two homes: Greece, where he was born and educated, and Canada, where he had become a citizen and taught the Greek language at the University of Toronto. When, after his death, I learned that he had named me a literary executor in his will, I thought first of the manuscript he had written about *Seferis and Friends* during those memorable warm Attic nights. I began editing it at once for publication. I edited only for continuity, and I did not change or omit any of his arguments or conclusions.

I would like to thank George Thaniel's sisters, Rica Nicoloulias and Mary Ruscillo of Toronto, for their encouragement and total support. It was George Thaniel's wish, made to me while he was living, that this monograph be dedicated to his niece and nephew, Debbie and Nick Ruscillo. Finally, I would like especially to thank Professor George Stubos (York University), a co-executor of Professor Thaniel's literary estate, for his very good advice and constant encouragement.

I present here for all interested readers my edited version of *Seferis and Friends*. If George Thaniel had lived, he would have felt immeasurable joy and satisfaction at its publication. I present it now as a tribute for my dead friend.

Ed Phinney
University of Massachusetts at Amherst
March 30, 1993

Chapter One

TWENTY ENGLISH LETTERS TO SEFERIS

INTRODUCTION

The Greek poet George Seferis (Nobel Prize for Literature, 1963) had an extensive and varied correspondence with many non-Greek writers, especially British, in the last 30 years of his life. Some of the letters he received and some of his own letters (barely legible carbon copies that he kept) have been printed in Greek translation, but the bulk of his correspondence remains unedited. The personal diaries of Seferis, of which we now have several volumes, help us understand him better as a man, as well as a poet and essayist. Indirectly, this is also true of the letters he received from authors and other intellectuals whom he happened to meet in his native country or other lands before, during, and after the Second World War. Many of these letters and, in some cases, Seferis' replies complement and amplify what we know about him and his work. They are also very interesting in themselves.

There are letters that add new and as yet little-known details of Seferis' life and contacts. For instance, Seferis' *Meres F* (56) provides only a brief, off-hand entry on Steven Runciman, the well-known Cambridge Byzantinist (now Sir Steven Runciman), with whom, in fact, Seferis had an enduring friendship and many productive exchanges. Runciman has donated Seferis' letters to him to the Seferis archives in Athens and written a brief account of his relationship with Seferis that sets the record straight, as it were, about Seferis the man. Runciman stresses that Seferis was not, in reality, the gloomy person that some people (inferring from his poems) imagine. Seferis had a lively mind and could share a good joke with a friend.[1] "But he was essentially a shy and rather private person," Runciman noted to the present writer, adding that Seferis grew more distant during the first part of his third extended stay in London when he was Greek Ambassador to Britain (1957-1962), a time of conflict between Britain and Greece over Cyprus. The political difficulties of that period, however, did not affect Seferis' personal friendships, with Rex Warner, for example, or Steven Runciman himself.[2]

One single letter, a witty but hurriedly scribbled note by Robert Graves that lies among the papers of Seferis, reveals that the two men knew each other and had probably exchanged books. Another single letter by A. Paulson, translator of August Strindberg into English, dated June 11, 1965, and addressed to Seferis while he was in New York, has to do with a proposal made to Seferis earlier that he translate into Greek Strindberg's Greek tragedy *Hermione* and have it produced in Greece— one of many such proposals made to Seferis after he won the Nobel prize. Seferis had declined, but Paulson wrote that he was still hopeful.

We know from Seferis' diary that Seferis first met Eliot and Auden at Stephen Spender's home (*Meres F*: 22); but it is also interesting to learn from Seferis' brief correspondence with Spender that Seferis stood as a referee for Spender who was seeking, in 1952, a teaching appointment in the English Department of the University of Athens. The exercise was unsuccessful, since the University chose Bernard Blackstone who, as Spender acknowledged, had stronger academic qualifications. The letter that Spender wrote to Seferis to thank him, all the same, was followed one year later by another, from the University of Cincinnati, United States, where Spender held a one-year appointment as Elliston Professor of poetry.[3] The letter speaks of a poem that Spender had written about Greece and that he wanted to dedicate to Seferis. This is "Messenger," in Spender's *Collected Poems* (189-190), a poem filled with allusions to Seferis' own poetry. In an early draft of Seferis' reply we read of the poem having "the right vibration" and a deep understanding of Greece. Seferis was proud of the dedication. The reply also makes it clear that Seferis was not happy in his new appointment at Beirut, though the troubles of the city were still in the future. In a radio broadcast in England shortly after the Nobel was awarded to Seferis, Spender had the opportunity to defend Seferis' work against "one or two unfavorable comments" that he had heard.[4]

When the present writer asked the retired classical historian A.R. Burn for permission to publish a letter that he had written to Seferis, Burn wondered when he had ever had "occasion to write a letter of any significance" to Seferis. Yet the letter that Burn subsequently remembered and kindly allowed to be published is significant in several respects: it provides some sober thoughts on the Cyprus issue, touches on the history and archaeology of Greece, and, above all, shows that a non-Greek is willing to return something ancient to its home in Greece, even if it is only a broken piece of hair from an archaic statue.

Burn met Seferis during the early part of the Second World War:

> I was first introduced to G.S.... in 1940 by L. Durrell... G. was then Foreign Press officer for the Athens Foreign Office [i.e., the Greek Ministry of Press and Information], and, as both he and nearly all the Greek press were pro-British, he had some reason during the German victories to be quite anxious. He said the German Press Attaché used to come every other day and roar at him. (E.g. "Read that! and now tell me, did we or did we not win the Battle of Flanders?" That was the one that ended at Dunkirk.) The Italian Press Attaché used to come twice a week and hiss at him, and his one consolation was that the British Press Attaché... only came about once a week and was quite nice! Well, we got him out in the end, as a high official and thoroughly compromised; and our old, slow, Polish ship was not bombed, probably because young Major (later Sir David) Hunt razzled up some Australian l-of-c drivers etc. and carried off 100 German shot-down aircrew... The German Ambassador watched the proceedings, and then no doubt telephoned Berlin via Bucharest![5]

Burn also adds that he sailed back to Greece, towards the end of the war, on October 22, 1944, on the same ship as Seferis. He recalls how, after reaching the Aegean, and all were "naturally hanging over the rails," Seferis came up from behind, threw an arm around him and said in mock-solemn tones, "Do you know? Not a single island has been lost!" as if the islands were ships or airplanes. Although Seferis has described, in much more detail, in *Meres D* (57-64), the 1941 "flight" to Crete on the Polish ship mentioned by Burn, the graphic points offered by Burn about those critical times are missing from Seferis' diary. Burn has added this comment: "Old Nestor lived to say in another war (*Iliad* 11.689): 'In those days we were few and hard-pressed in Pylos.' So were we in 1940; and yet, somehow, those were the days!"[6]

Lawrence Durrell, who introduced Burn to Seferis, was close to Seferis, at least during the early years of their friendship, and this is shown by the letters the two men exchanged as well as by references to Durrell in Seferis' diaries. Durrell was also responsible for the acquaintance of Seferis with the only American writer who preoccupied him in any sustained manner, Henry Miller. Although Ezra Pound and T.S. Eliot also came from America, Seferis considered them as European rather than American writers.

We do not know how close Seferis' association was with the American poet and dramatist Archibald MacLeish, but probably not very close. MacLeish praised Seferis highly, nevertheless, when in 1965 he gave his opinion on Seferis to (the journalist) Elizabeth Kray, saying that Seferis was "not only a great poet *in* this time— which would be wonder enough," but he was "also a great poet *of* this time."[7] Two years later, MacLeish dedicated his poetic drama *Herakles* to Seferis and we have the first draft of Seferis' response to this gesture. The MacLeish letter printed below comes from an earlier period. It was sent to Seferis when he was still stationed in London and suggests that the two men had either met at least once before or that they had exchanged some kind of correspondence.

Of particular interest, naturally, are the letters that touch upon Seferis' work. The great majority of his English-speaking friends read his poetry in translation. A few could read it also or primarily in Greek. Romilly Jenkins was teaching Greek at King's College, University of London, when he received and read, with an obvious scholarly interest, the first Greek edition of *Thrush*. In his letter to Seferis, Jenkins seems to resist the poem's highly allusive and arcane character, but finds an interesting parallel between the words spoken by the "Socrates" of *Thrush* and some by King Lear in Shakespeare's play, as well as an echo of late Latin poetry at the end of Seferis' poem.

Maurice Bowra was in America delivering the Charles Eliot Norton series of lectures for 1948-1949 ("The Romantic Imagination"), when he wrote to Seferis, on October 12, 1948, to thank him for the gift of *The King of Asine and Other Poems*, responding at the same time, somewhat lightheartedly, to the sense of exile that many of Seferis' verses evoked: "Like you, I am an exile... It [i.e., America] is all another world and not what I know. Even the birds and flowers are different, and the country, though beautiful, has no gods." Bowra's reaction to Seferis' *Poems* was also brief, with a comment on the "infernally difficult" act of translation (letter of November 10, 1960). Seferis must have enjoyed the literary aspect of Bowra's brief description of the English summer of 1964 in a letter he received from Wadham College (where Bowra was the warden), in Oxford, shortly after that University had conferred on Seferis an honorary doctorate: "Real, Shakespearean summer is on us here— blinds down, windows open, the smell of flowers, all very somnolent and agreeable." The words contrast vividly with a more practical note sent, a few months earlier, to Seferis from Bowra on what clothes Seferis would need to wear at the ceremony relating to the honorary doctorate mentioned above. In 1970, Seferis contributed 50 pounds towards the creation of a new quadrangle at Wadham College in honor of Bowra who was then retiring. Both men died in 1971, Bowra preceding Seferis by three months. Seferis mentioned Bowra twice in his *Dokimes*, the second time comparing him to Eliot: Bowra's effusive temperament contrasted with Eliot's circumspect manners.[8]

Benjamin Britten seems to have received or read his copy of *Poems* (1960) with some delay. In his letter of thanks, he sounds decorous about the translations and provides some interesting autobiographical details. The single letter from Robert Graves to Seferis, which was mentioned earlier, also touches on the translation of Seferis' poems, quoting what has become by now a cliché, Frost's statement that "poetry is what gets lost in translation." It may be worth noting that in 1963, when Graves was Professor of Poetry at Oxford, he was asked his opinion about whom the Nobel Prize for Literature should go to and he recommended Frost. The Swedish Academy chose Seferis. The paths of Frost and Seferis crossed for a third time, in a context unrelated to Graves, in Rachel Hadas' book *Form, Cycle, Infinity: Landscape Imagery in the Poetry of Robert Frost and George Seferis*.

When E.M. Forster died at age 91, in 1970, Seferis wrote a kind of obituary, "E.M. Forster: A Look from the Leaning Tower," (*Dokimes*, II: 333-338), which traces in simple and warm-hearted tones the chronicle of his friendship with the English writer and liberal thinker. What must have attracted Seferis to Forster particularly was the fact that Forster had been the first non-Greek European to notice the poet Cavafy. This special interest was also shown in the presentation by Seferis to Forster (at the celebration of his eightieth birthday in King's College, Cambridge, in January, 1959) of a Hellenistic coin of King Demetrius Soter illustrating a poem by Cavafy. The coin is now displayed at the King's College Library, together with the original of a Seferis letter to Forster (dated October 16, 1959). The card beside the coin reads: "A Greek coin presented by Seferis to E.M. Forster, on his eightieth birthday, in memory of Cavafy. Tetradrachm: Demetrius I, Soter (162-150 B.C.), son of King Seleucus Philopator, to illustrate Cavafy's poem 'Of Demetrius Soter.' January 9, 1959."

"Often do I peruse that coin," Forster says in the postscript of a letter to Seferis published here together with a second, earlier letter in which Forster acknowledges his receipt of Seferis' *Poems*. Forster is forthright in saying that he could not have "the complete key" to these poems since he had no mastery of modern Greek. Seferis must have also appreciated Forster's speaking concretely about his poetry, starting from a specific point in the collection.

Poems had very good reviews in England and was awarded prizes that had been reserved, up to that time, for English poetry. R. Graves, G. Barker, and W. Snodgrass earned, in 1960-1961, Guinness poetry awards. In addition, at the request of the judges, special awards of 50 pounds each were made to D. Walcott and Rex Warner. In Warner's case, the item honored was the translation of Seferis' "The King of Asine" (in *Poems*). Much more important was the awarding to Seferis himself, as author of *Poems*, of the Foyle Prize for poetry. This was the first time the prize was awarded to a non-English poet, as the letter of Christina Foyle announcing the award explains.

The translator Rex Warner (poet, novelist, and scholar) must have felt vindicated for his hard work. As director of the British Council in Athens in 1945-1947, he had known Seferis well. Seferis had lectured at the British Council and flown kites with Warner's small son on mountain slopes around Athens. Warner wrote the introduction to *The King of Asine and Other Poems*, and in the 1950s he worked on his own translations of Seferis with the help of the poet and of George Savidis, who was to become the main editor of Seferis' works in Greece. Many of Warner's letters to Seferis from that period have to do with these translations.

Seferis' relationship with Warner survived the storm which, in the meantime, had erupted between England and Greece over the Cyprus issue.

"I don't know whether you are back from America yet or not, and I follow the news with the kind of distaste that you can imagine," Warner wrote in 1957, at the height of the crisis. In February, 1957, Seferis and other Greek officials were at the United Nations in New York, with the purpose of defending the Greek position in the debates over the Cyprus conflict. Warner illustrated his words with a reference to a poem by Seferis: "No need to mention it. You've said most of the important things in 'Salamis in Cyprus.'"

After the Cyprus issue was or seemed to be resolved and *Poems* had appeared in print, followed by the success described above, the two men could correspond unencumbered by political burdens. In a letter that seems to post-date the awarding of the Nobel prize to Seferis, Warner spoke of an article on Seferis that the editors of *Life* had solicited from him. He also announces that he had been offered a well-paying job at the University of Connecticut. The topic of the article in *Life* comes back in a Warner letter from early 1964: "The nice girl there (who rewrote most of what I said) promised to send you copies. I think that my own style of writing is a bit better than hers, but, on the other hand, she invented that fine Homeric adjective 'mule-traversed,' simply because I told her that you liked islands where there were more mules than motor-cars."

In a letter dated March 12, 1964, Warner said that on his way back from Princeton (where he presumably gave a lecture or did something academic) he was going to see Auden in New York, adding: "I'm still terrified of New York and can really only contemplate it from the sea and, as it were, *sub specie aeternitatis*."[9] By May, 1964, Warner seemed established at Connecticut: "Yesterday I had the task of introducing Marianne Moore to an audience here. She is 77 years old and very charming. I've returned from Buffalo where I read some of your poems almost within sound of Niagara Falls." Other letters of this period touch upon the topics of Seferis' accepting the honorary doctorate at Oxford ("I'm glad that Oxford is catching up with Cambridge.")[10] and Warner's plan to translate into English a selection of Seferis' *Dokimes*. The plan materialized in *On the Greek Style*.

Several poets, Greek and non-Greek, dedicated poems to Seferis, and he inscribed some of his own poems to others. But Warner seems to have been the only person celebrated by Seferis, in a poem written for a special occasion, Warner's sixtieth birthday in 1965. "Letter to Rex Warner, resident of Storrs. Connecticut. U.S.A. On his sixtieth birthday." (now in *Collected Poems*:

333-337) traces some of the landmarks in the friendship of the two men that started in Greece just after the Second World War:

> [...]
> We were walking in a country ruined by the war,
> where they'd crippled even the dolls of children.
> The light, quick and strong,
> bit into everything and turned it to stone.
> We walked among
> bicycles and kites,
> we watched the colors but our talk
> strayed to that restless horror.
> [...]
> Now, among the tentacles of this great city
> I think about you once again.
> Everything's television,
> you can't touch things easily at close quarters.
> In the heat of this electric night,
> in loneliness unbreakable as the sea-floor's,
> the illuminated skyscrapers
> show their windows gleaming
> like the skin of a huge sea monster
> as it breaks clear above the surface.
> The many-colored crowd that filled them,
> the measureless jostling crowd,
> has moved on by this time
> to other pleasures and other anxieties.
> [...]
> Now you are sixty
> and I can't offer you anything
> but this idle chirping.
> Still, I feel that I'm encircled and goaded on
> by a flock of philetaerous sparrows.

The "great city" likened to an octopus in the poem is of course New York City, some of whose great museums were visited by Seferis, as is evidenced by the part of the poem not quoted above. Seferis was in America in June, 1965, primarily to accept an honorary degree from Princeton, when he started the poem to Warner. A note that Seferis appended to the poem suggests that he finished it three years later, in the winter of 1968, when he was again in America as guest of the Princeton Institute for Advanced Study.

The background of that second trip to America was this: in 1966 Seferis was made an honorary member of the American Academy of Arts and Sciences, and in 1967 he was invited to become Charles Eliot Norton Professor of Poetry at Harvard for 1969-1970. Though honored, he had to turn down the invitation for reasons of conscience. He thought that if there was no freedom of expression in his own country, where the Colonels had taken power in April, 1967, there could be no such freedom anywhere in the world, for him at least. He could not see himself lecturing freely at Harvard when several Greek intellectuals were either in jail or unable to write or publish freely in Greece. He accepted, however, the invitation from Princeton to become a fellow of the Institute for Advanced Study in the last quarter of 1968.

At Princeton Seferis worked on an old project of his, the study and translation of Platonic myths, and at the same time he gave readings of his poetry at various universities in the United States with the assistance of his translator, the creative writer and scholar E.M. Keeley, who also interviewed him for *The Paris Review*— that conversation is now included in Keeley's *Modern Greek Poetry*. The poetry reading of Seferis in New York was introduced by Eugene J. McCarthy, the poet, scholar, and politician who ran, a few years later, in 1976, for the presidency of the United States as a liberal independent candidate. McCarthy was senator from Minnesota when the Colonels seized power in Greece in 1967, the year he published his book *The Limits of Power: America's Role in the World*. He was critical of the American administration's tolerance, if not approval, of the Greek dictatorship and sympathized with George Seferis when the latter issued his now famous protest in 1969 against the Greek regime. In fact, Seferis' decision to break his silence over politics and make that protest may have resulted from his meeting people like McCarthy during the 1968 visit to America and his being pressed by audiences to air his view of the political situation in Greece.[11]

In "Reflections on George Seferis,"[12] McCarthy explained the circumstances of his writing a poem and dedicating it to Seferis. When he was thinking of Seferis' poem "In the Manner of G.S." (*Collected Poems*: 107-111), McCarthy happened to read in the *New York Times* about the impending tour of various allied countries, including Greece, of the American warship *U.S.S. Constitution*. This inspired him to write "Jumping Ship," a poem critical, in metaphorical terms, of his country's attitude towards what had happened in Greece. Then he used some lines from Seferis' poem as an epigraph to his own and to accord it its poignant conclusion. That was in December, 1968, when Seferis was still in America. The letter of McCarthy published here dates to more than a year later, but starts with a reference to McCarthy's "Jumping Ship," which Seferis, in the meantime, had translated into Greek.

Another person who used verses by Seferis in her own work was the Marchesa Iris Origo, writer of historical novels and studies. John Murray's letter, published last in the selection, informed Seferis of Origo's wish to use some of his poetry in translation in one of her books. From the first draft of a reply, we know that Seferis gave permission for the quotation and was slightly amused by Murray's letter, that reminded him, as he said, of Stendhal, more particularly of Stendhal's heroine Sanseverina in *The Charterhouse of Parma*. Sanseverina was a duchessa rather than a marchesa, but she was also a writer. We may infer, then, that the name and title of Iris Origo contributed to Seferis' associating her with Stendhal and the Romantic period.

Any survey of the letters that Seferis received from his English-speaking friends and, above all, the letters themselves, testify to the great range and depth of the Greek poet's correspondence with his non-Greek peers over a fairly long period of time. The letters presented here confirm our image of Seferis as a keen and alert observer of the world and of man's inner universe. It is not he who speaks, yet we learn much about him through these letters. They are part of his life.

NOTES

1. Sir Steven Runciman, "Some Personal Reminiscences," *Labrys*, 8 (April, 1983), 47-49. Personal recollections about Seferis are also included in Ph. Sherrard, "The Death of a Poet: the Poetry of George Seferis," *The London Magazine*, 12, 4 (1972), 6-22, and in P. Leigh Fermor, "The Art of Nonsense" (review of Seferis' *Piimata me Zografies se Mikra Pedia* (Poems with drawings for little children)), *Times Literary Supplement*, January 26, 1977. See also A.R. Burn's reminiscences of Seferis above, pp. 12-13.

2. In a letter to the present writer, dated December 20, 1978, in which Steven Runciman replies to a request for an opinion on Seferis.

3. Spender held various other teaching appointments in the 1960s, presided over the English Center of International PEN, and was Professor of English Poetry at University College, London, between 1970 and 1977. He was knighted in 1983.

4. A typescript of the speech with handwritten corrections is found among the papers of Seferis.

5. Letter to the writer, dated May 22, 1986.

6. Ibid.

7. A copy of MacLeish's letter, addressed to Elizabeth Kray (but with no other indication), is found among the papers of Seferis.

8. *Dokimes*, II: 333-338. Bowra figured also in the P. Leigh Fermor review cited above (note 1).

9. Cf. Bowra's reaction to the American landscape, p. 14-15 above.

10. Cambridge had been the first university, in any country, to bestow on Seferis a doctorate *honoris causa*. Oxford and the University of Thessaloniki followed in 1964, Princeton in 1965.

11. See John E. Rexine's article, "The Poetic and Political Conscience of George Seferis," *Modern Greek Studies Yearbook*, 3 (1987), 311-320.

12. *Modern Greek Studies Yearbook*, 1 (1985), 145-151.

TWENTY LETTERS

From John Lehmann,   12 May 1947
London, England,
To George Seferis,
Athens, Greece.

My dear George Seferis,

I am sending you a copy of Demetrios's book, which we have just brought out, as I promised.[1]

It would interest me enormously to know what you feel about it: perhaps you could find time one day to write to me about it. I think everyone who has seen it over here agrees that it is quite unique, the impact terrific when one reads all the poems and articles together. You will know better than any of us to what extent this Demetrios is different from the Demetrios you knew before the war in Greece.

Rex [Warner] will, I hope, have told you how delighted I am to be publishing your beautiful new poem. I shall be writing to you about your book very soon.[2]

With all good wishes.

John Lehmann

[P.S.] What about Cavafy and Eliot? I have not forgotten you promised to let me see a translation of that.[3]

---

1. Demetrios Capetanakis, who died young (1944), grew up in Greece but learned English so well after moving to England, that he could be mistaken for an English writer. His close friend John Lehmann published his writings, poems, and essays, in a memorial volume titled *Demetrios Capetanakis (a Greek Poet in England)* (London, 1947).

2. The "beautiful new poem" must be *Thrush*. The book in question is *The King of Asine and Other Poems*.

3. Seferis' comparative study of Cavafy and Eliot, "Cavafy and Eliot— A Comparison" (*On the Greek Style* 121-161).

From John Lehmann,   19 November 1947
London, England,
To George Seferis,
Athens, Greece.

My dear George Seferis,

I was very glad indeed to have your letter about Demetrios's book;[1] do you know, I had heard nothing at all from Greece since I sent the book off in May to a large number of addresses (including Canellopoulos)[2] and was finding the silence rather extraordinary. Then, only a couple of days after your letter came one from Dr. John, Demetrios's brother, so perhaps the books were very much delayed in reaching Athens after all.

The book had a rather restricted sale, but quite extraordinarily interesting and appreciative reviews. I cannot help feeling that the interest will gradually grow as the years go by. I am particularly anxious to hear how the critics treat the book in America, when it is published over there; there is already a considerable interest in certain literary circles.

I was very happy indeed to read all you had to say about it, and do very much hope that you will be able to write that longer piece you mention in the not too distant future.

We did indeed receive Ghika's drawing for the frontispiece of *The King of Asine*,[3] and are very glad to have it. The book has gone rather slowly, I'm afraid, through the process of production, but it should be ready early next year (with luck). I do hope you will like the look of it.

I was extremely sorry to hear how ill you had been, and send you all my sympathy. I do hope your recovery is complete and lasting.[4]

With all good wishes, and many pleasant memories of our meeting this time last year.

Yours sincerely,
John Lehmann

1. See note 1 of previous letter. Regarding Capetanakis' mastery of English, Kenneth Young noted that C. "wrote as well in English as he did in his native language," in "The Contemporary Greek Influence on English Writers" (*Life and Letters*, 64 (1950), 56).

2. Panayotis Kanellopoulos, well-known scholar and politician, had been a teacher and close friend of Capetanakis.

3. *The King of Asine and Other Poems.*

4. Seferis underwent a rather difficult kidney operation in 1947. (See *Meres E.* 111-117).

From Romilly Jenkins,   27 June 1947
London, England,
To George Seferis,
Athens, Greece.

My dear Mr. Seferis,

I received your exquisite poem *Thrush* from Mr. Valaoritis[1] yesterday. I have already read it three times, with very great enjoyment. I think the second section, B, the best, perhaps because I understand it best. One of the disadvantages of much modern poetry lies in the poet's free and, in some cases, apparently whimsical use of erudite allusion, which, even when partly explained by notes, renders it hard for the reader to follow. But a sound classical education helps me in this case, though I doubt if I should have recalled the Aeschylus passage without your note to "Soulmonger."[2]

By the way, at "And if you condemn me, etc."[3] have you in mind Lear's terrific line "If you have poison for me, I will drink it"... and the *Pervigilium Veneris*[4] at "Whoever has not loved..."?[5] No matter, it is the province of great poetry to set up these allusive vibrations in the mind, whether consciously or not. The Homeric introduction to the very un-Homeric similes on pp. 14, 15, is graceful.[6] I think perhaps the "Radio" is the "clou" of the whole,[7] but it's all very fine. Thank you so much.

I shall be in Athens in September; I should so much like to meet you.

Yours sincerely,
Romilly Jenkins

1. The poet and scholar Nanos Valaoritis, then a university student in England, translator (with L. Durrell and B. Spencer) of Seferis' *The King of Asine and Other Poems*.
2. *Poems*: 98, 124; *Collected Poems*: 331, 542.
3. *Poems*: 99: "If you sentence me to drink poison..."; *Collected Poems*: 333: "And if you condemn me to drink poison..."
4. "The Vigil of Venus," a late Latin poem.
5. *Poems*: 101: "He who has never loved shall love..."; *Collected Poems*: 339: "Whoever has not loved will love..."
6. Reference to the first section of Part II of *Thrush* (in the first, Greek edition of the poem, 1947), *Poems*: 95; *Collected Poems*: 323.
7. *Poems*: 97-98; *Collected Poems*: 327, 329, 331.

From Stephen Spender,   3 May 1952
St. John's Wood, N. W. 8.
Maida Vale 7194, England,
To George Seferis,
London, England.

Dear Seferiadis,

I think you may have heard by now that the philosophical dept. of the University of Athens chose Professor Blackstone and not me last week.[1] The decision is not quite final, because it has to go through the Senate and also because there may be complications on the side of the British Council. But I do not know about this.

In any case I wish to thank you very much for your kindness, generosity, and sympathy. I would like also to tell you how I feel about the matter.

The University was quite justified in deciding that I have very few academic qualifications. For this I blame only myself, and it is painful to me to think that when I was younger I did not take the trouble to acquire those degrees etc. which would make it quite clear to people in authority that I could undertake a teaching job of this kind. Perhaps I regret this even more than my political indiscretions.

Not to go to Greece is disappointing to me in a way which only people who feel that in some way Greece is the one place they have always belonged to, can understand. When I was there last week I wondered why I had ever gone to any other place abroad, and now I feel that no other appointment would mean anything to me except as a means of eventually getting to Greece. However, perhaps feeling in this way that one is part of Greece is a complicated matter, not just settled by going to live there for a few years. Possibly it is in my work that I should and can belong, and the deeper disturbance which I feel at present, is realizing that I haven't deserved to belong yet. At all events during these few last days in Greece before I knew what had been decided I felt that in a larger sense than things which Professors decide, I had not really earned an appointment in Greece. And perhaps if I ever do earn it, then the work and the satisfaction will involve more than just going there.

It is difficult to express such thoughts, but I feel you are the one person who may understand them.

Thanking you once more for seeing above all that my idea was that I had both something to give and something to take which might have made me become a poet in a sense which I have never as yet felt myself to be.

Yours very sincerely,
Stephen Spender

1. See Introduction, p. 12.

From Stephen Spender,   4 March 1953
Cincinnati, Ohio, U.S.A.,
To George Seferis,
Beirut, Lebanon.

Dear Mr. Seferis,

I have written a poem about my love for Greece. It was really inspired by my longing to live there and the hope that I might do so. Before writing to you, I have sent this poem to several of my friends and they all seem to think it worthy of the honour I now ask: which is to dedicate it to you. I hope you will not object to my sending it for publication to *Botteghe Oscure* with this dedication.[1]

It was sad to miss you in London. I shall be at this address until the end of May, if you would be so kind as to write me a line here. Please remember me to Madame Seferis.

Yours sincerely,
Stephen Spender

1. See Introduction, p. 12.

From Steven Runciman,   16 April 1953
Thessaloniki, Greece,
To George Seferis,
Beirut, Lebanon.

My dear George,

I ought to have written long ago to thank you for all your kindness at Beirut. It was a real joy to see you again and it greatly added to the charms of Beirut— otherwise a slightly charmless city.

The Easter weekend at Constantinople was impressive. The Patriarch performed the ceremonies with a sense of serious drama that I found moving.[1] The Congress [of Byzantine Studies] here is rather overwhelming, but excellently organized— far too many parties and receptions, but all given *con amore*, so that the atmosphere is full of welcome. I am fond of Salonica, a city of the "Great Ideal."[2]

I saw George Katsimbalis for a moment as I passed through Athens. He seems to have been in a difficult mood lately but seems now to be brighter and happier, much more the Colossus that we used to know.[3]

I will write again when I get home.

My love and gratitude to your wife.

Steven

1. Reference to the Ecumenical Patriarch Athenagoras the First.
2. "Great Ideal": the ambition of the modern Greek nation to liberate from alien rule all those areas, beyond its borders, that were Christian and Greek-speaking. Thessaloniki (Salonica) had been outside Greece's borders before 1912.
3. George Katsimballs, close friend and patron of Seferis, hero of Henry Miller's book *The Colossus of Maroussi*.

From Steven Runciman,   30 December 1954
St. John's Wood, N. W. 8.,
Cunningham 0010, England,
To George Seferis,
Beirut, Lebanon.

My dear George,

My young nephew, Garry Runciman (of whom I may have written to you before), will be passing through Beirut at the end of next week; and I have told him to go and see you as I should like him to have the privilege of knowing you. He is young, not yet 21, but extremely intelligent and rather serious— rather too serious, I think— and mercifully quite unspoilt in spite of a brilliant scholastic and social career at Eton. I am very fond of him, and so I shall be very grateful indeed for any kindness that you may be able to show him.[1]

I meant to write to you some weeks ago, to thank you for your letter about my *Crusades*, Vol. III.[2] What gave me real pleasure were your words about the rhythm of my style. It is my ambition to get the rhythm of the prose right at the significant points; and it is so difficult to know if one has succeeded, especially as it is a thing that critics never seem to notice, or at least never mention.

On January 15 I am flying to the Far East to spend two months in Siam, Malaya and India. I have not been very well, and I want to find sunshine and heat, in an atmosphere completely different from that about which I write, before I start on another book.

With all good wishes for 1955 to Maro and yourself.

Steven

1. The Seferises did receive Garry Runciman, and the latter wrote to thank them, on January 10, 1955, from Amman, Jordan.

2. *A History of the Crusades*, in three volumes (1951-1953), is Runciman's principal work. Volume Three is subtitled "The Kingdom of Acre and the Later Crusades."

From Sir Steven Runciman,   6 December 1959
St. John's Wood, N. W. 8.,
Cunningham 0010, England,
To George Seferis,
London, England.

My dear George,

The Anglo-Hellenic League is holding its Annual Meeting on Wednesday, January 13 (at 5:30 p.m., I think— but details will be sent later—) and we much hope that you will both of you come to it.[1]

The Committee has also asked me to ask you if you would come in a private capacity as well, and read some of your poems to the meeting. I said I thought there were few things that you would like to do less and that I thought it an impertinence to ask you. However, I must do what my Committee says and ask you— and, certainly, could you face the ordeal, nothing would give us all more pleasure. But I for one will not be surprised if you firmly say no.[2]

I am just back from a fortnight of pleasant and solitary quiet in Scotland.

Yours ever,
Steven

---

1. From a letter of Sir Steven Runciman to the writer: "You ask about the Anglo-Hellenic League. It is our British-Greek friendship society— non-political and non-official, but with a certain semi-official status— founded in the 1920s and still going strong. It was my task to keep it going during the difficult years of the Cyprus dispute." Runciman presided over the society from 1951 to 1967.

2. In the draft of a brief response to the above letter, Seferis writes: "I enjoyed your charming understanding of the human heart. I explained, yesterday, to two or three ladies of your Committee that I couldn't add the ordeal of reading poetry to my present occupations."

From Sir Steven Runciman,   11 February 1967
London, England,
To George Seferis,
Athens, Greece.

Dear George,

It was kind of you to send me your piece on Dante: which I have read with enormous interest— almost with annoyance because it has made me go and read long passages of the *Commedia* when I ought to have been working on other things. You have helped me to see much that I had missed in it. I am very grateful.[1]

Will you be in Athens March 21-26 when I shall be briefly there, staying round the corner with Mark Ogilvie Grant? I hope so. I wish I were staying longer; but I have to hurry on to Constantinople and then hurry back to Scotland, as by then, I hope, they will be fitting bookcases into my ancient tower and I must be there to watch over it all.

Steven

---

1. Reference to Seferis' essay on Dante, "Sta 700 Hronia tu Danti" (On the 700th Anniversary of Dante), in *Dokimes*, II: 249-282.

From Rex Warner, 15 February 1957
Oxford, England,
To George Seferis,
Athens, Greece.

My dear George:

I seem to have lost my pen. This makes for legibility.

I don't know whether you are back from America yet or not,[1] and I follow the news with the kind of distaste that you can imagine.

No need to mention it. You've said most of the important things in "Salamis in Cyprus."[2] I think that the enclosed version of this poem is an improvement on the first, and I hope that you will agree.

I've just had a long letter from Savidis, who, from his letters, seems a most charming man.[3] He has sent me a number of new literal translations, and I'm looking forward to trying to avoid mutilating them. At least I can understand "Quiet, Rex!"[4] Meanwhile old John Lehmann (Aphrodite?) has managed to get away with "Helen,"[5] and it should appear in *The London Magazine* before long. Thank God he didn't print that awful translation by...

There are many things that I should like to say, but they must wait for happier times, if, as I can imagine you writing, times do get happier. But here it is rather a question of the conjunction of appropriate occasions. These seldom occur.

We both send our love to you and Maro.

Rex

1. Seferis and other Greek officials had gone to the United Nations to defend the position of the Greek government in the Cyprus conflict with Britain. Shortly after that, Seferis was named Greek Ambassador to England.
2. *Collected Poems*: 383-387; *Poems*: 110-112. Seferis' poem is an indirect indictment of the then official British policy seeking to deny or change the Greek character of Cyprus. See Chapter Three, pp. 92-96.
3. The Cambridge-educated George Savidis, critic and scholar, who was to become the main editor of Seferis' works.
4. A self-deprecating comment by Warner. "Quiet, Rex" is an admonition addressed to a dog in Seferis' poem "In the Kyrenia District" (*Collected Poems*: 523).
5. *Collected Poems*: 355-361; *Poems*: 114-116. Lehmann getting hold of Seferis' "Helen" and publishing it, is paralleled to the goddess Aphrodite, who promised Helen to Paris and helped him kidnap her.

From A.R. Burn,   20 September 1954
Glasgow, Scotland,
To George Seferis,
Beirut, Lebanon.

My dear Seferiades,

This is to say that Mary and I really hope we may get a chance of visiting Syria and Lebanon next spring! The way we hope to do it is as guides to a party of tourists; this arises out of a tour which we took to Greece last month; they were very nice "serious" people, and I think we may say without exaggeration that the trip was a success, and that any trip like it does some small service to international understanding. Incidentally, I took them to Asini.[1] I hope very much that we may be able to see you and Madame Seferiades, some evening when we abandon our "flock," if we are lucky enough to be in any of your "capitals" at the same time as you.[2]

I have just been trying to get into touch with a young Anglo-Greek named Stephanou, who was in our Consulate in Damascus when I was in Syria in 1942-3; but he is not in the F.O. List, so presumably has left the service. I thought he might be able to give us useful advice on somebody who would take on the business of hotel-bookings and chartering of motor-coaches, etc., and could be relied on not to promise more than he could really do! I suppose none of your staff have come across him? Incidentally, if any of your staff could themselves recommend a local travel agent or agency, preferably in a smallish way of business (so, they are more likely to give personal attention to things), and if they could be good enough to write me, I should be much obliged. As you know, my wife and I can get along well enough in Greek or French, and would very willingly work with any Greek who had your recommendation. But the nationality is a secondary business, so long as the man will not promise the impossible in an effort to please a prospective customer![3]

The party, if it materialises, will probably also look in in Cyprus for a few days on the way back, and I think I can promise you that that part of the trip also will improve the party's understanding of the situation if we have the guiding of it. I really do think intelligent British opinion has moved quite a lot lately; though of course unintelligent opinion always counts more noses. But I find the prolonged history of the Ionian Island agitation a comforting parallel these days.[4]

I hope you and Madame are well. We are; though I am afraid

the same cannot be said of my mother, who is now 88, and whose condition gives us some anxiety.

I do hope we may see you next spring.

Yours ever,

A.R. Burn

---

1. In the Argolid, Greece; setting of Seferis' "The King of Asine."
2. Seferis was posted in Beirut but represented Greece also in Syria, Jordan, and Saudi Arabia.
3. It has not been confirmed (though an effort was made to that effect) whether Burn's project was really carried out.
4. Allusion to the Cyprus issue. See Introduction, p. 13, and Chapter Three, pp. 92-96. The Ionian Islands were ceded to Greece by Britain in 1864, peacefully, but after a prolonged agitation.

From A.R. Burn,   13 June 1957
Glasgow, Scotland,
To George Seferis,
London, England.

My dear George,

if we may still call you so in your present grandeur![1]— This is, first, to say how glad we are that you should be back in London again; and that while we regret as much as anyone the present trickiness, as you must find it, of your post, I am sure that never was there a time when your special gifts and knowledge of Britain had so much chance to do good. Public opinion here, as you know, is not immovable, and I am sure you will find many opportunities to contribute to good relations between our countries (I do not presume to speak of your official duties), both in conversation about the present unhappy public affairs with people who wish to talk about them and are amenable to argument, and in literary or other harmless talk with people who are not usefully to be approached with any reference to present issues.[2]

Mary and I hope you will manage to carry out your hoped-for

visit to Scotland this time, and if we can help to show you Glasgow or Loch Lomond, or this University,[3] we shall of course be more than pleased.

And now, second, I have a real piece of news: I have an actual bit of Greece, if only a wee one, *toso mikro mikro*,[4] to return to its mother country and its proper place; I am sorry it is not either Cyprus or the Elgin Marbles,[5] but as you know, if I do not return those it is only because I have not got them.

Nearly thirty years ago, on my first visit to Greece, I scrambled down from the *Kolonnes* at Sounion[6] to have a swim at the bottom, and half-way down I picked up a piece of worked marble, about 7 inches long. I thought it was some sort of architectural fragment, though I could not remember ever seeing anything quite like it. I must confess that I took it home in my pocket without an export licence, and hope that I shall not be arrested next time I set foot in Greece now that the truth is out. I can only plead in extenuation that if I had not picked it up, it would probably before long have gone into the sea.

Only lately, while showing my little collection of bits and pieces to some students who are hoping to visit Greece soon, it occurred to me, since I still could not compare it to anything architectural, to wonder if it could be a bit of a sculpture; and one of my students said "Could it be a bit of hair?" This put me on the track. It is *not* like most archaic hair, but I turned up Gerke's photos of the great Sounion Kouros[7] — and lo, its hair is treated in an unusual way, concave where most archaic hair is convex and vice versa; and that *Kouros* has a chip of hair missing beside its left ear, which appears to be exactly the size and shape of my fragment. It was probably overlooked and thrown out with the débris when the Sounion statues were dug out of a pit (where they may have been stowed after being knocked down by the Persians, like the Acropolis Korai)[8] in 1906. The chip is very much reddened by contact with the earth on the broken side, so it has probably been detached since ancient times (480 B.C., in fact?). It is going to be a great pleasure to restore it, as soon as I have had a photograph of it taken for a small paragraph in the *Journal of Hellenic Studies*, which Gomme has asked me to write.[9] Either I can take it myself when I go to Greece with a party of tourists in August, or deliver it to you for transmission by bag. I only hope that this may be an omen of more important future events.

I hope Madame l'Ambassadrice is well and enjoying the prospects of your new appointment. We shall hope to see you in London if we may call some time this summer. Mary joins me in all our felicitations and good wishes.

Yours sincerely,
Robin Burn

1. Seferis was named Ambassador of Greece to Britain in May, 1957.
2. Allusion to the conflict between Britain and Greece over the Cyprus issue.
3. Burn had been lecturing at the University of Glasgow since 1946.
4. "Such a little thing."
5. The Parthenon Marbles displayed in the British Museum, in London. Known as "Elgin Marbles" from Lord Elgin, ambassador of Britain to Turkey, who was responsible for the seizure and transportation of the sculptures to Britain in the early 1800s.
6. The Temple of Poseidon at Cape Sounion, in Attica.
7. The statue can be seen in the Athens Archaeological Museum.
8. These archaic statues of young women, now restored from fragments discovered in a pit and displayed in the Acropolis Museum in Athens, should not be confused with the more famous Caryatids.
9. A.R. Burn, "A Fragment of Sculpture," *Journal of Hellenic Studies*, 78 (1958), 13. The brief article describes Burn's *trouvaille* and announces its restoration to where it had come from, a spot "above the left shoulder" of the Kouros of Sounion.

From Morgan Forster,　　　　　　30 November 1960
Cambridge, England,
To George Seferis,
London, England.

My dear George Seferis,

It was a great joy to receive your poems with their affectionate inscription.[1] I have been reading them as one does poems to which one doesn't and can't have the complete key; a key being only complete when it includes mastery of the original language. I read them some time back, but little passages continue to hover: the sentence, for instance, which says that one is no longer free to choose one's own form of death.[2] I think this profound as well as disquieting. As I get older I assume that certain forms of death— painful and ignoble ones— can be dismissed, and that without having lived like Oedipus I can select my end.[3] The assumption is baseless.

　　I hope that you are well and I shall have the chance of seeing you again soon.

　　Yours affectionately,
　　Morgan Forster

1. See Introduction, pp. 15-16.
2. Forster is probably alluding here to Seferis' *Mythistorima*, 22, which ends with the dramatic question: "Shall we be able to die in a normal way?" (*Poems*. 30), or "Will we be able to die properly?" (*Collected Poems*. 55).
3. Oedipus is apotheosized in Sophocles, *Oedipus at Colonus*.

From Morgan Forster, 20 May 1961
Cambridge, England,
To George Seferis,
London, England.

My dear George Seferis,

What a pleasure to get your letter. This is to say that I am getting better in a slow and almost dignified way.[1] If you ever are in Cambridge and have a spare moment, I needn't say how delighted I should be to see you; or perhaps we may get [to] meet again in London.
    Yours affectionately,
    Morgan Forster

P.S. Often do I peruse that coin.[2]

1. Forster was being hospitalized at the Addenbrooke's Hospital.
2. See Introduction, pp. 15-16.

From Christina Foyle, 17 January 1961
London, England,
To George Seferis,
London, England.

Your Excellency,

I believe you know that my father gives a prize of £250 every year to the author of the most outstanding volume of poetry published.[1]

    He would very much like to present the prize on his birthday, which is in March, at a Literary Luncheon. We should be so delighted if you would be our guest of honour on Friday, 3rd

March, at the Dorchester Hotel, to receive the annual Foyle Poetry Prize.

My father made this award to encourage poets and among writers who have received it are Dylan Thomas, Walter de la Mare, Dame Edith Sitwell, John Betjeman, and Christopher Fry.

We do not announce the name of the winning poet until the luncheon and I shall be most grateful if you will keep it a close secret.

This year, it will be a specially delightful occasion as it will be the first time that the prize has been awarded to a poet who is not English, and we all hope very much indeed that you will be able to come to the luncheon.

Yours sincerely,
Christina Foyle

---

1. The brothers W.A. and G.S. Foyle founded W. and G. Foyle Booksellers in 1903. Christina A.L. Foyle, daughter of W.A. Foyle, joined the company in 1928; began Foyle's literary luncheons in 1930; started the Book Club with her father in 1937; and directed Foyle's Lecture Agency.

From Robert Graves, 26 November 1961
Oxford, England,
To George Seferis,
London, England.

Dear George,

I tried to bring you flowers this Monday— "few, certainly, but roses"[1]— to the London clinic where your Press people said you were, but on my arrival it was said that you were not there, even under an alias, so I sadly took the flowers to an old Jewish friend at the Middlesex Hospital.

This is to thank you most warmly for your poems and the inscription. Although Robert Frost defines poetry as "what gets lost in translation," a great deal came through, perhaps as the result of my meeting you personally and getting your personal rhythm conveyed to me.

I hope you are well soon. I'm off in a very short time to my home in Mallorca [Majorikë] which is said to have been colonized by Lindos of Rhodes— and I think that this may well be true.

Yours,
Robert Graves

[P.S.] Back in June.

---

1. Greek, in the original. This was said about Sappho's poems by the Hellenistic poet Meleager. See D.L. Page, ed., *Epigrammata Graeca* (Oxford, 1975), 248.

From Archibald MacLeish,   4 April 1962
New York,
To George Seferis,
London, England.

My dear Ambassador:

I am writing (in the hope that you will remember me) to say that one of your most distinguished *American* countrymen, Elia Kazan,[1] the stage director and motion picture director and producer, will shortly visit London with the principal object of seeking your advice on a matter of first importance to him.[2] He is a very dear friend of mine, having directed my play *J.B.* in New York, and I feel sure you will enjoy talking to him if you can make time for it. This brings you, as always, my deep admiration and friendship.

Faithfully,
Archibald MacLeish

---

1. Elia Kazan (shortened form of Elias Kazanjoglou) was descended, like Seferis, from a Greek family of Asia Minor (Turkey).

2. The matter referred to here may have had to do with Kazan's movie *America America*, which was partly set in Turkey.

From Benjamin Britten,   3 March 1963
Aldeburgh, Suffolk, England,
To George Seferis,
Athens, Greece.

My dear George Seferis (because that is how I think of you):

Please forgive the disgracefully late acknowledgement of your poems. Since we left Greece (the day the book arrived) both Peter[1] and I have been followed by a series of minor disasters— an accident on the snowy slopes in Switzerland had landed me in plaster, cancelled a German tour, and makes me go tomorrow for a concert tour of USSR on crutches!— and our lives have been very disorganized. But please accept here my belated thanks for your much treasured present. I am delighted to have your poems, and signed with such a charming dedication. I have read them with the greatest pleasure, especially (as you guessed it would) the evoking of a familiar and beloved landscape in "The King of Asine."[2] The translations read to me very convincingly; I wonder what you feel about them, with your strong views on translation.

    It was also a very great pleasure to spend that evening with you, at the Closes. I do hope it will not be very long before we meet again, either in England or Athens. Do let us know if and when you pay this country a visit.

    In the meantime, my very best wishes for further great creative impulse! It gives us such richness. And many thanks again for the poems, and from Peter for his exquisite Delphic book.[3]

    Yours sincerely,
    Benjamin Britten

1. Peter Pears, opera singer and life companion of Britten.
2. *Poems*. 71-73; *Collected Poems*. 265-271.

3. Most probably, the German edition of Seferis' *Delphi*, a travelogue that he wrote in 1961, for the Knorr und Hirth publishers. This work was printed, in a translation by Isidora Kamarinea-Rosenthal and with photographs by Herbert Kreft, in the series "Das Kleine Kunstbuch."

From Eugene J. McCarthy,   24 March 1970
Washington, D.C., U.S.A.,
To George Seferis,
Athens, Greece.

Dear George:

It was very good to receive your letter with the translation of "Jumping Ship" in Greek,[1] and I am sorry to be so slow in answering it.

I wish that the reports on the government in Greece were more encouraging and that there was a deeper interest in the United States in restoring liberty in your country. I have been in Russia and in Ireland since I last saw you. In Russia, I saw Andrei Voznesensky, the poet. You may have read that his new play, which is really a blend of verse, music, and dance to some of his poems, has been closed down by the Cultural Bureau of Russia. It was allowed to run only two nights. He was hopeful when I talked to him that it would obtain their approval but it did not.

In Ireland, I met Austin Clarke, one of their oldest poets, whom you may know.[2]

There is, I think, a temptation to write poems about animals but perhaps it is a temptation to which one should yield. I am enclosing a copy of the article from *Look* as well as two poems I have done. "Ares" has been published in *McCall's* magazine here.

[...]

With best wishes,
Sincerely yours,
Eugene J. McCarthy

1. The translation is included in Seferis' *Tetradio Yimnasmaton*, B (Book of exercises, B).

2. There is a poem titled "To Austin Clarke" in McCarthy's *Ground Fog and Night* (New York: Harcourt, Brace, Jovanovich, 1978).

From John Murray,   20 April 1970
London, England,
To George Seferis,
Athens, Greece.

My dear George,

I hope you will forgive me bothering you with a request but, in any case, it gives me the opportunity of sending you greetings and saying that it is far too long since we met.

The request is to ask you for your approval for the use by the Marchesa Iris Origo of the following quotation which is a Walter Kaiser translation from a poem of yours:

> ... as pines
> keep the shape of the wind
> even when the wind has fled and is no longer there
> so words
> guard the shape of man.

Iris Origo would so much like to use this quotation to head a chapter in her autobiography entitled "Reading and Learning," and we publish the book this Autumn. May we have your approval? Acknowledgement would of course be made.[1]

Iris Origo is in London for a few days and she asks me to say how very much she would like to have an opportunity of meeting you when you are in Rome. I do hope such a meeting might be possible...

Love to you both,

yours ever,

Jock

P.S. John Betjeman lunches with me tomorrow and I know he would send his love also...

1. The Seferis quotation from *Three Secret Poems* appears as the epigraph of Chapter 6, "Reading and Learning," in the Marchesa Origo's autobiography, *Images and Shadows: part of a life* (London: J. Murray, 1970).

Chapter Two

SEFERIS AND ENGLAND:
A GREEK POET IN AN ENGLISH LANDSCAPE

The special relationship which George Seferis developed with Britain in the last 40 or so years of his life is obvious even to the casual observer of his life and work. He started and finished the foreign part of his diplomatic career in London, and on various other occasions, before, during and after the Second World War, he had to deal with British politicians, diplomats and military officers. He developed a close tie with T.S. Eliot, but he had many connections with other influential English writers as well. It would be fair to say that without the publicity that these writers provided for his literary work and the honors which he received in Britain towards the end of his career (1960-62), the Swedish Academy could not have known enough about Seferis to consider him a candidate for the Nobel Prize for Literature and finally to give it to him in 1963, the first Greek writer to have received it.

The connections of Seferis with England and the English intelligentsia were celebrated, after his death, by exhibitions held in Athens and London, the eulogies which British friends published on his behalf, and the scholarship which his poetry and his other work generated in the English-speaking world. One might add that the associations of Seferis with North American intellectuals and institutions seem really to post-date the awarding of the Nobel prize and may be seen as extensions of his long-standing ones with Britain. These facts are fairly obvious; yet, apart from Seferis' associations with the poetry and critical thought of Eliot, there has never been an attempt, beyond generalities, to explore them. The topic has many ramifications and should be meaningful to comparatists as well as English and Greek specialists.

In this chapter, I will investigate Seferis' reactions to the natural and human landscape of England in the formative years 1931-34, when he served his country as acting Consul General in London; in the summer of 1944, when Seferis flew to England from Egypt, carrying certain messages to the British

Government from the Greek Government in exile; and in the period 1951-52, when Seferis served again in the Greek Embassy in London, as First Counsellor.

Seferis was born in Smyrna, in Asia Minor. He was raised both there and, subsequently, in Athens, and for the rest of his life he remained an emotional captive of the Greek landscape with its frequent views of the sea. Seferis was born in 1900, on February 29 by the old Greek Calendar (March 13, by the new). Many of the happier notes in his poetry are related to the sea. The diaries reflect this fascination with the sea more directly: "My second swim at Vouliagmeni. *Magic* of the sea hard to explain. How it changes me all at once: my wonder, a wonder deep to the bone. I cannot understand. I should go closer, I should try to cross that borderline into another world" (*Meres E*: 33).

Between 1918 and 1924 Seferis studied in Paris and, although he sometimes felt emotionally alienated, he loved the city and its rich cultural atmosphere. "I spent six and a half years in Paris," Seferis noted in his diary. "I lived fully and wholeheartedly, loving each moment, each corner of the city and each stone" (*Meres B*: 80). In the second half of 1924, after he had received his diploma in law, Seferis traveled to London with the purpose of learning English, as his family wanted him to become a diplomat. His earliest poem, "Fog" (*sic* in the original), dates from those days. The younger sister of Seferis, Ioanna, had already received from him letters with descriptions of foggy days in Paris (Tsatsos 1982: *passim*), but it was London, on Christmas Day, 1924 (hence, probably, the caricature of angels in the second and third stanzas) that inspired Seferis with a poem on the subject of fog, a meteorological phenomenon rather rare in Greece.[1]

FOG
say it with a ukulele

"Say it with a ukulele..."
grumbles some gramophone;
Christ, tell me what to say to her
now that I'm used to my loneliness?

With accordions squeezed
by well-dressed beggars
they call on the angels
and their angels are hell.

And the angels opened their wings
but, below, the mists condensed,
thank God, for otherwise they'd catch
our poor souls like thrushes.

And life's cold as a fish
— Is that how you live? — Yes, how else?
So many are the drowned
down on the sea's bed.

Trees are like corals
their color gone,
carts are like ships
sunken and lonely...

"Say it with a ukulele..."
Words for words, and more words?
Love, where's your church,
I'm tired of this hermitage.

Ah, were life but straight
how we'd live it then!
But it's fated otherwise,
you have to turn in a small corner.

And what corner is it? Who knows?
Lights shine on lights
pallidly, the hoarfrosts are dumb,
and our soul's in our teeth.

Will we find consolation?
Day put on night—
everything is night, everything is night—
we'll find something, if we search...

"Say it with a ukulele..."
I see her red nails—
how they must glow in firelight—
and I remember her with her cough.

This poem, which partly rhymes in the original and has naturally lost part of its charm in the free verse translation, well suggests, *à la manière de* Corbiere and Laforgue, the young poet's relation to London in winter, and also reflects an attitude which Seferis continued to express, with variations of tone and color, in the remainder of his work. It is a critical attitude towards life. Yet, though the tone in "Fog" is mordant and self-deprecating, it is not as yet tragic.

Six years passed before Seferis saw London again. In 1931 he was posted to England, to serve in the Greek consulate. He sailed to Marseilles, toured Southern France in a French colleague's automobile, took the train to Paris where he saw a performance of dances from Indochina (part of the Colonial Exhibition of '31), and proceeded to London, arriving on Monday, August 17. "Green grass and smells of bacon," he noted in his diary (August 24), "I have the impression of spending the night locked in a room filled with flowers. I cannot breathe very well." The frequent rain depressed him. "In the room next to mine a phonograph is heard. The panes in my window where the rain is beating are startled every so many minutes by the subway" (September 12). "Is it the voices of our dead friends? The phonographs persist. Each room here seems to have a phonograph that serves, on black disks,[2] Spanish and Negro tunes" (September 20). Three months later, Seferis, too, procured himself such an instrument in order to hear his favorite music, Franck, Debussy, Stravinsky, and— one presumes— jazz, which he also liked very much. "He [Seferis] knew every [jazz] virtuoso of any account; he was a subscriber to 'Le Jazz Hot' I soon discovered," Henry Miller wrote in *The Colossus of Maroussi* (1941: 107). Miller met Seferis in Athens, in 1939, but the craze of Seferis for jazz dated from his London days, as he himself has informed us in "A Conversation with Seferis" (Keeley: 201).

Soon after his arrival, Seferis moved to Hampstead, a district of London, as boarder of an old widow and her chain-smoking and ever-coughing daughter. He took care to describe his new surroundings and daily routine in letters to Greece. He spent many hours every day at his desk, alone, reading and writing. What he saw from his window is sometimes described in terms worthy of Evelyn Waugh: "A feeble sunshine touches my desk. A few minutes ago as I was putting on my clothes, I could see through my bedroom window two plump Amaltheias playing tennis. Two mobile castles. The little ball was Ariel: light, agile, it made fun of them" (May 28, 1932). By "Amaltheias" Seferis meant of course "she-goats." In Greek myth, Amaltheia was a female goat who nursed the infant Zeus. Seferis used the animal image again, 20 days later, in a different context: "It has not stopped raining for the last fifteen days. If the theory about the environment is true, then the English should be frogs" (May 28, 1932).

The image of a different world often entered Seferis' mind: "A small house among the pines, basil plants in the pots, and white-washed walls, and at the foot of the hill the great world open to all directions" (September 20, 1931).[3] Later, when he woke up one December morning and felt trapped by the solid cold, he hallucinated a blazing noontime sun in Athens, solid "like a piece of bread." But Greece was on his mind for other reasons as well. Before leaving for England, Seferis had published in Athens his first book, *Turning Point*, and was ruminating on the reactions of critics and friends, several of them negative. Imagery from those poems came to haunt his new impressions from London: "Today, Sunday, I stayed indoors for the whole day. The air outside was filled with fog: you could not see two yards before you. Now, in the evening, the street lamp looks totally alienated— like that ship of Arthur Gordon Pym.[4] I understand the Spaniard who took such a lamp inside his room to give it protection" (November 29, 1931). The Spaniard was Ramon Gomez de la Serna, a surrealist about whom we hear in *Meres D* (283).[5]

Seferis was still under the spell of French culture. He listened mostly to French music, read French writers, spiced his letters with French quotes, and thought that if he had good company he would have liked to spend New Year's Day in Paris. The river Thames was inevitably compared with the Seine:

> This afternoon, about 3:30, I walked down to the river. It is the only area which I like unreservedly, and I am sorry that its embankments are not longer, as in Paris, so that I could follow them for two hours on foot. This would have given me a big rest. The river does not look at all like the Seine; it is much wider and succeeds in giving you the impression of being part of the sea which is nearby. The bridges are enormous and shake in the centre, the current looks swifter and more in tune with the sky, which it caresses, in the evening (for this is the impression I get). If I were not a little nervous, I could have stood for hours, looking at the illuminated ads that puncture the fog or, further down, the tug boats which look from the distance like a black island, an ungoverned mass. You must have seen paintings of Whistler or Turner. Add a note of Bach and you will be able to visualize the scene I am describing.
> (December 16, 1931)

Here is a man who has seen many works by the Impressionists in Paris (Manet, Monet, Renoir) and some in London and who does not overstate his description of landscape. A poem that Seferis wrote about the same time shows his love of economy and precision more fully:

Hampstead

Like a bird with broken wings
that had traveled through wind for years
like a bird unable to endure
tempest and wind
the evening falls.
On the green grass
three thousand angels had danced the day long

naked as steel
the pale evening falls;
the three thousand angels
gathered in their wings, became
a god
forgotten
that barks
alone
and searches for its master
or the Second Coming
or a bone.
Now I long for a little quiet
all I want is a hut on a hill
or near a seashore
all I want in front of my window
is a sheet immersed in bluing
spread there like the sea
all I want in my vase
is even a false carnation
red paper wound on wire
so that the wind
the wind can control it easily
as much as it wants to.
The evening would fall
the flocks would echo descending to their fold
like some quite simple happy thought
and I would lie down to sleep
because I wouldn't have
even a candle to light,
light,
to read.

"Hampstead" is a remarkable poem which, as Vayenas (53) aptly has observed, combines realism and symbolism in equal amounts. This combination was made possible, in part, because the English landscape that Seferis was describing was less familiar to him and he felt the need to be accurate in its description. On the other hand, his recollections of the Greek scenery did not relate to a specific locale, but to a hypothetical one. The balancing of two different landscapes against each other accords the poem a certain pleasant rhythm.[6]

Seferis' need to escape the London air, however, involved much more than hypothetical Greek landscapes. Listening to Stravinsky's *Rite of Spring*, Seferis remembered Nijinsky (who had danced it) and composed a long poem in prose, "Nijinsky," describing a dream in which he had seen the famous dancer go through a symbolic ritual. "Hampstead" and "Nijinsky" and other poems of this period belong in a series of poems supposedly written by Stratis Thalassinos (Stratis the Mariner, or Sailor), a persona that Seferis had used to represent a more adventurous, aggressive, and realistic part of his personality, his Odyssean self, so to speak. The name may have been "given" to Seferis by *The Arabian Nights* on the analogy of Sinbad the Sailor. Seferis' other, more self-conscious self, was composing, or at least trying to finish a more lyrical, rhymed poem, *The Cistern*, which he had sketched while in Greece and which, when finally published in 1932, was thought by critics to be a Greek equivalent of Valéry's *Le Cimetière Marin*, just as Seferis' *Erotikos Logos* (part of his collection *Turning Point*) had been taken to be a Greek analogue of Valéry's *La Jeune Parque*.

The problems that Seferis experienced in his effort to secure the uniform tone of a symbolist, typical of Mallarmé or Valéry, in *The Cistern*, remind us of the epigraph from Pindar: "There is a most vain class among men which, despising ordinary things, fixes its eyes on distant things, pursuing empty air with idle hopes..." (*Pythian Odes*, 3: 21-23), which Seferis had attached to his *Erotikos Logos*. The suspicion that Seferis had when attaching this, namely that he was pursuing something out of tune with his time and everyday experience, grew stronger as he tried to rework and polish *The Cistern* in London. He had changed, or at least his perception of things had changed, and in a very human way he blamed the environment: "Pure lyrical poetry does not go well with London: I cannot sing: I have no tune, if you like" (May 28, 1932). His discomfiture had to do with the daily habits of his landladies:

> I was awakened at 8 by the phonograph of my houseladies and then kept on edge by the vacuum cleaner. It sounds like a street drill. Every morning the same old story. The phonograph is a new problem. About a fortnight ago, the ladies obtained the recording of a song from a musical review and now they suck at it like candy. The old lady wakes up in the morning on that and the daughter goes to bed in the evening on the same. I am trying to come to terms with their perception of music. They consider me a fool for the music I buy, I mean the simple works like Franck's *Symphony* and Granados' *Dances*; they find them most unusual. (Naturally, when I am to play [Stravinsky's] *Rite of Spring* or Satie's *Gymnopédies*, I double lock myself in). (May 8, 1932)

Seferis was making a resolute effort, at this time, to update himself musically, by going to concerts and writing subtle analyses of what he heard in letters he sent to a female friend well versed in music. Several of Seferis' poems had their origin in his favorite musical pieces, and R. Beaton may be right in suggesting that in a 1931 entry of *Meres B*, where Seferis recounts an idea of a piece of music, "The Watch and the Expedition of the Argonauts," we have a foreshadowing, in musical terms, of what later became the poem-sequence *Mythistorima*.[7] Many years later, he became friends with Igor Stravinsky, a composer he had always admired, and wrote a fine introduction to Stravinsky's *Poetics of Music*, a reprint of the Charles Eliot Norton Lectures that the Russian composer had given at Harvard before the Second World War.[8]

In the middle of May, 1932 Seferis was overwhelmed by the torrential English spring that he could not help comparing with the leaner spring of Attica. Again his descriptions of the nature around him are impressionistic and studded with felicitous similes:

> In the morning I took a long walk in Regent's [Park]. You felt the invisible sun pressing upon the clouds which, in their turn, were weighing upon the people. On the living grass, children, dressed in bright colors, looked like wooden toys. One child pretended to be

dead while the others threw on his body handfuls of grass and earth, until some rogue of a child picked up a brick which he dropped on the belly of the dead child, who was resurrected at once with tears. Further down, a small white-clad Japanese girl was hopping like a chickpea; alone, like an exiled haiku.
(June 12, 1932)[9]

In July, 1932 Seferis moved his residence from Hampstead to an apartment attached to the Greek consulate where he now had increased responsibilities. To combat boredom and give at least verbal form to things which concerned him, he composed haiku:

> When the haiku came out all right, I felt relieved, as if all those spiders, labyrinths, and "the ineffable" things of a blind life were transformed, for a moment, into something real— a pine needle or a beach pebble, let us say, into seventeen syllables. I dare tell myself that the problem [of life] is not harder than the problem of a haiku.
> (July 23, 1932)[10]

On his first anniversary in England, Seferis counted the pros and cons of the year:

> [I am left] with two things: the flame and the river... Here I set about trying to know this country better, to learn the language at least. I heard the best music of Europe. I visited superb museums. Books can be read anywhere. But I missed the company of people, the freshness and stimulation of human contact. I came to know the ordinary people, but I was not able to know the better ones. My type of work does not offer any intellectual environment and indiscretion is not my forte. After all, the best artists here are thought of as silly or scandalous, and those interested in them "high-brow"— an untranslatable and forbidding word. I happened to scandalize some decent gentleman by referring (in passing) to Byron! You would not dare to say anything about Lawrence or Joyce, who wrote books now forbidden. Well,

the big city; that is something. To learn a language; that is also something. And to earn your living without being a burden to someone; that is certainly something. There is my balance.
(July 23, 1932)

The passage is straightforward and speaks for itself. As for the "flame and the river," think back to the poem "Nijinsky" that Seferis was inspired to write by contemplating the flames of his fire at Hampstead and to his description of the river Thames. The "flame" and the "river" are also symbols that Seferis found in the poetry of Eliot, and that he used in his own way more than once. In fact, one could see in this oracular summing up of Seferis' gains from his first year in England, an allusion to Eliot, who is not named in the diary entries of 1932, although verses from Eliot's "Ash Wednesday" were quoted once (September 18, 1932), after the laconic introduction: "When I returned home, I read some English poems."

From other sources, Ioanna Tsatsos' *My Brother George Seferis* and the correspondence between Seferis and George Theotokas, we know that Seferis was preoccupied with Eliot throughout 1932, and in an essay that he wrote many years later, "Letter to a Foreign Friend," (*On the Greek Style*: 166), we learn the circumstances of his first coming upon Eliot's poetry shortly before Christmas 1931. The question is: why did such a capital event not find its way into Seferis' diary? There are possibly two answers. The first is given by Seferis himself in his *Meres* C (178), where he states that a diary is hardly all our moments, or the essence of our life, but merely "the trace, almost accidental, of any given moment, now and then, and not always of the most significant moment" (March 3, 1940).[11] The second is that for many months, perhaps for more than a year, Seferis was not exactly sure of the significance of his discovery and the impact it was going to have on his own work. Perhaps it was Eliot's essays, in which Seferis found many of his own thoughts on poetry clarified, that attracted Seferis first.[12] The poet Eliot's dramatic manner of expression and stylistic innovations took more time to work their influence on Seferis.

When Seferis wrote to George Theotokas on August 20, 1932 (Seferis-Theotokas: 116-117), he quoted some lines from Eliot's "The Hollow Men," but did so for emphasis. His mind was still preoccupied with the two series of poems he wanted to complete and publish after *The Cistern*. We have already referred to these poems, starting from "Hampstead," first in the series *Five Poems by Mr. Stratis the Mariner*, and "Nijinsky," last in the series *Mr. Stratis the Mariner Describes a Man*. Seferis says to Theotokas:

> I have also started something. It has been dragging along since last October... If it materializes, I will feel much relieved. But I do not dare to think about what is going to happen with the public and the critics. If it does not materialize, I will be very unhappy, mon cher chevalier.
>
> Between the conception
> And the creation
> Between the emotion
> And the purpose
> Falls the shadow
>
> says Eliot.

Moreover, the incompatibility that Seferis still found, towards the end of 1932, between himself and the English environment, was evident in the humorous entry for October 17, the last substantial entry of the year:

> Stratis the Mariner... came up to tell me:
> — You know, I have found one of the serpents of *Erotikos Logos*.[13]
> He opened a newspaper and read: "10 snakes free." Then, in the same manner:
> — And the important thing is that it spoke to me. Yes, Sir, it spoke:
> "*Erotikos Logos* is lying; it was not two serpents; it was a single one, I!"
> I begged him not to bother me. He left whispering:
> — O.K., O.K., goodbye! If you do not believe me go and

find out for yourself. But you must hurry, I am not sure you are going to catch it in time. In the paper that he threw on the table I read:

"They say that it cannot live for long in the cold night air and that although it is strong enough to kill a goat in its native country it has no future in England."[14]

And yet, it had, if we take the "serpent" to be Seferis himself, who simply took time to acclimatize himself in England. If, however, we take the "serpent" to be an allusion to the erotic self of the poet, it is another story. In any case, towards the end of 1932, Seferis was still concerned with his published work and felt like a stranger in England.

Before we consider the seminal year of 1933, in December of which Seferis started writing his first major work, *Mythistorima*, we should look again at those poems, in his collection *Book of Exercises* (published in 1940), which were "given" to the poet before 1933. "Reflections on a Foreign Line of Verse" takes its cue from Joachim du Bellay's poem "Les Regrets," especially its first line: "Heureux qui comme Ulysse a fait un beau voyage." On first view, this poem would suggest the use of the "mythical method" that Seferis had already used, if unconsciously, in an earlier poem, "The Companions in Hell" (in *Turning Point*).[15] But the "mythical method"— which, as the present writer believes, Seferis consciously adopted only after he had observed it in Eliot— works here only to a degree, since the bond between the hero, Ulysses, and the modern poet, who sees his life unfolding along Ulyssean lines, is not a complete identification but a commonplace resemblance. On the other hand, the English ambience is slight, and we may feel it, for instance, behind lines such as "sometimes when I sit surrounded by exile I hear its distant murmur like the sound of sea struck by an inexplicable hurricane," where "its" refers to the love or lust for life that the hero possesses when he sets out on his long voyage. The Ulysses who appears to comfort the despairing narrator of the poem is not Cavafy's compulsive traveler and refined hedonist (poem "Ithaki"), but an old, seasoned man with a white beard and hands "calloused by the ropes and the tiller, his skin weathered by the dry north wind, by heat and snow," and has come to tell the narrator (who is to be identified with the poet) how he may build his own wooden horse to capture his own Troy. This poem, which was noticed and discussed by W.B. Stanford (1954: 177-178), is quite removed from the playful and *fantaisiste* poems (*à la* Paul-Jean Toulet) of *Turning Point*, and may be said to prefigure, particularly with its last lines, the sombre imagery of much of Seferis' later poetry. The new, realistic and dramatic mode that Seferis developed while in England is evident, to a degree, in this poem.

Reviewing the 16 haiku printed in *Book of Exercises*, we may stop at this one:

> Is it the voice
> of our dead friends or
> the gramophone

which was "given" to Seferis by a popular English song, as his diary suggests;[16] and the following, especially titled "In the Museum Gardens":

> Empty chairs:
> the statues have gone back
> to the other museum

where the museum alluded to might be in London or anywhere. What is more remarkable here is the use of "statues" in the sense of the "living dead," an image that recurs in Seferis' poetry.

"Hampstead," first in the *Stratis the Mariner* series, was discussed earlier. The second brief piece in the series may be an autobiographical sketch of Seferis the acting Consul General:

Psychology

> This gentleman
> takes his bath each morning
> in the waters of the Dead Sea

then dons a bitter smile
for business and clients.

The image of "flame-gazing" found in the poem "Nijinsky," seems to start the series *Stratis the Mariner Describes a Man*, also in *Book of Exercises*. The man who sits, every afternoon, "staring at a flame," and is now confiding to Stratis the Mariner, is of course Seferis' other, more intimate self, who reviews his life starting with his childhood. But this is not strictly an autobiographical poem in spite of its personal tone. The speaker and confessant is rather a composite representative of a whole generation of Greeks who grew up with Seferis and had to face the same disillusionments and withstand similar pressures. The speaker is a sensitive and exacting individual who has tried to secure a foothold in the quicksands of modern history. This desirable and finally identifiable *pied d'appui* is the "flame," a symbol of balance between memory and forgetfulness:

> What can a flame remember? If it remembers a little less than is necessary, it goes out; if it remembers a little more than is necessary, it goes out. If only it could teach us, while it burns, to remember correctly.
> (5. "Man")

In the beginning of 1933 Seferis' morale was rather low, if we judge from his diary. He was not amused even by a letter that he received, as consul, in which the writer, unknown to him, wanted to be informed why a column of the temple of Olympian Zeus in Athens had collapsed sometime in the last century, while the others were still standing, and inquired whether he could obtain a photo of the fallen column.[17] The diary entries and letters, which Seferis sent to Greece during this period, were nervous and, at times, delirious. As he said, he missed companions and human affection. We also suspect that Seferis was disappointed by the reactions of critics and friends in Greece to *The Cistern* and uncertain about his poetics, finding himself at a crossroad, between *poésie* pure, represented by his poems *Erotikos Logos* and *The Cistern*, and realism, which at this time was reflected in the *Stratis the Mariner* poems. Seferis agonized à la Mallarmé ("le papier vide que la blancheur défend") over the blank paper: "Midnight. Early in the afternoon, it was snowing heavily; the roads were slippery. The paper is now for me like the glass that fishermen use to scan the depths of the sea" (February 23, 1933).

But a bell had rung. Seferis was reading Eliot's poetry and essays more and more, finding many of his deeper concerns and aspirations spelled out in Eliot's work, but all the time resisting Eliot's religious mysticism. He wanted to meet Eliot and asked a Greek friend who knew the English poet to write a letter of introduction on his behalf. But Eliot was away in America for the Charles Eliot Norton Lectures at Harvard. The two men finally met as late as 1951, and many years later, in 1967, Seferis himself was asked to deliver the same prestigious series of lectures for 1969. He declined, however, with the argument that it would not be proper for him to lecture and teach outside Greece, when many other men of letters were not allowed to do the same inside Greece (which, at the time, was under the dictatorial regime of the Colonels).

Seferis' interest in Eliot was made evident in the April 15, 1933, entry of his diary, an entry weighed down with facts and ideas that would appear in verse as well as critical essays in years to come.

> Yesterday I listened to Handel's *Messiah*. I also read a lot of Eliot and thought about him. I should start an essay on Eliot. I would touch upon the issues that interest me, although I regret that my knowledge of the English language and literature is inadequate. I know things which nobody else in Greece knows, and this man interests me. Last year I thought that he was the first poet whom I have influenced! I could not explain this similarity in our inclinations and quests in any other way. The truth is that we both had the same teachers in a period which counts: Laforgue, Corbière, etc... Last night, I threw on paper about thirty lines of *The Waste Land* in [Greek] translation. It would be a tour de force for someone to translate such a work. But I will pursue it.

The relationship of Seferis to Eliot has been a prominent issue with Greek critics and has been discussed from various angles, with or without apparent bias. Some British and American scholars have also devoted serious thought to the issue. Here, let it suffice to say that sometime *nel mezzo del camino* of his life and in an alien environment, Seferis was able to see beyond his personal problems and beyond the English landscape itself, natural and human, into areas as yet half-realized in his mind. He did so with Eliot as his guide, just as Dante had done something similar many centuries earlier, with the help of another poet, Vergil:

> I spent three entire days alone in the [Easter] holidays. I did not feel bored, although I went out very little. Something is being fermented inside me. I may be deceiving myself. Anyway, the wind has changed direction, from denial to affirmation.
> (April 17, 1933)

Two weeks later, Seferis sailed upstream on the Thames, to Hampton Court, but bothered by the large crowds of people, returned almost immediately, looking at the green banks of the river and the other boats sailing by. He liked what he saw and remembered some of Spenser quoted by Eliot in *The Waste Land*: "Sweet Thames, run softly till I end my song,/ Sweet Thames, run softly, for I speak not loud or long." He noted that he had seen Eliot in a dream the previous night.

Eliot does not reappear in the few remaining entries of Seferis' 1931-34 diary, which ends with Seferis' return to Athens, by ship, in February, 1934. The few entries mirror a familiar Seferis who went to theatres and concert halls and described, in minute and often picturesque details, both the ambience and the performance— he particularly liked an evening of Indian music and dancing, while he felt uneasy about Wagner— and who took solitary but equally observant walks in parks and around the historical areas of London, such as Chelsea, commenting on the old houses of eminent writers and artists of the past, watching the anonymous crowds act out various parts in the tragic comedy of life:

> How to go about liking this city? It lacks shape. Sometimes, however, it grows into a music of architectural bulk, strength of buildings, and

hospitals. The river holds the line of the melody.
(November 22, 1933)

There are poems written during this period that compensate for the scarcity of the diary entries and, moreover, suggest the ways in which Eliot's themes were skillfully woven into the fabric of Seferis' art. The series of poems *Notes for a "Week,"* written in the summer of 1933 and subtitled "British grown daffodils," are in terms of articulation and imagery Eliotic, in contrast to the *Stratis the Mariner* poems where no Eliotic influence is apparent. The new series, also in *Book of Exercises*, has been given scant attention by critics, probably because for many years the series was not known in its complete form,[18] and because of the intensely private character of these poems, hard to understand without some explanatory notes. More than any other poems of Seferis, *Notes for a "Week"* are products of the English environment with which Seferis was gradually coming to terms in 1933. In "Monday," the initial image of the "blind" sleeping "among the bending asphodels" is developed around a parenthesis: ("I remember the paphiopedilums of another winter/ enclosed in the hothouse heat. Enough of Life"),[19] that capitalizes on part of the diary entry of March 13, 1933:

> Yesterday I went to Kew. The spring, what they call here "crocus time," was beautiful... I tried to get into the small enclosure of the paphiopedilums, but the huge crowd and the stench together with the heavy air of the hothouse made me giddy.

We could also compare the following entry from the diary:

> It is eight in the evening; there is still some light outside. I drew my curtains apart, as far as they could go. I have just turned on the light. From my window I see, across from me, a most classical-looking pediment, colour of a dove breast. Paintings of De Chirico.
> (June 17, 1933)

with its compression in these verses from "Sunday":

> Soon it'll be dark; I see a pediment of amputated statues still looking at me. What do statues weigh?

The pictorial impression of the diary entry has become here a haunting image with overtones of tragedy and double entendre. The broken statues symbolize a dead and useless past, on the one hand, and the living dead of today, those whom Seferis saw in his walks in the streets of London and in the subway and whom he found walking across the London bridges in Eliot's *The Waste Land*.

One whole poem from the series reveals, better, Seferis' new and freer technique:

Thursday

I saw her die many times
sometimes crying in my arms
sometimes in a stranger's arms
sometimes alone, naked;
so she lived near me.
Now at last I know there's nothing further
and I wait.
If I'm sorry, it's a private matter
like the feeling for things so simple
that, as they say, one's passed beyond them;
and yet I'm sorry still because
I too didn't become (as I would have wished)
like the grass I heard sprouting
one night near a pine-tree;
because I didn't follow the sea
another night when the waters were withdrawing
gently drinking their own bitterness,
and I didn't even understand, as I groped in the damp seaweed, how
much honor remains in the hands of men.

All this passed by slowly and conclusively
like the barges with faded names:
HELEN OF SPARTA, TYRANNUS, GLORIA MUNDI
they passed under the bridges beyond the chimneys
with two stooping men at the prow and stern
naked to the waist;
they passed, I can't distinguish anything, in the morning fog
the sheep, curled, ruminating, barely stand out
nor does the moon stand out above
the waiting river;
only seven lances plunged in the water
stagnant, bloodless
and sometimes on the flagstones, sadly lit
under the squint-eyed castle,
drawn with red and yellow pencil:
the Nazarene, showing his wound.
"Don't throw your heart to the dogs.
Don't throw your heart to the dogs."
Her voice sinks as the clock strikes;
your will, I sought your will.

"Mixing memory with observation"— to paraphrase Eliot— Seferis has brought together, here, material of varied provenance, following a method of free associations, enlarging the scope of the poem from the personal to the universal as he allows images from the Greek and the British landscapes to creep into his poem. "Don't throw your heart to the dogs./ Don't throw your heart to the dogs" may be the exhortation of a preacher whom Seferis encountered in a London street. This is also a variation of a Gospel passage: "Give not that which is holy unto the dogs" (Matt. 7:6). As for his picture of the Nazarene, it is the reflection of an incident that Seferis has related elsewhere.[20] The last line also has unmistakable biblical overtones, and we may further recall that Thursday, in the Greek Orthodox tradition, is the day of Christ's crucifixion.

In *Notes for a "Week,"* Seferis does not borrow any unassimilated imagery from Eliot. He was too intelligent for that. He was simply encouraged, by the example of Eliot's poetry, to mix together what we could call his older "baggage of images" (from the Greek and French cultures) with the new impressions he obtained from the London, and more broadly, English environment, and to follow a stream-of-consciousness technique that becomes more evident than in his previous poetry. In the title, the word "Week" is intentionally placed within quotation marks to distract us from the notion that we have here seven separate poems, each one written on a different day of a particular week. *Notes for a "Week"* is, on the whole, a transitional piece of work for Seferis, on his way to conceiving and writing his first truly mature work, the 24 piece *Mythistorima*.

The two and a half years that George Seferis spent in England, between 1931 and 1934, were for him an undoubtedly formative period. He even came to like London, at least partially, in the few months that preceded his return to Athens. He seems to have enjoyed the spring of 1933 and the contemporary London scene and felt depressed when, for a while, he was in danger of being posted to Cardiff. "I did not enter the Diplomatic Service in order to be a Harbour Master for four years," he wrote, somewhat bitterly, to his sister (Tsatsos 1982: 212), and it is probably this problem, among others, which prompted him to make, to George Theotokas, the following comment on some Athenian critic's pseudo-grand utterance ("je suis un homme en proie au temps et au problème total"): "Moi," Seferis said, "je suis un homme en proie au mauvais temps (I am in London, after all) et aux problèmes partiels" (1975: 126).

The second half of this period was quite removed from the time of Seferis' early lyrics— this, in fact, he admitted to his sister (Tsatsos 1982: 211)— but it was also removed even from the beginning of his stay in London, when he was trying to translate Valéry's essay *Propos sur la poésie* (Ibid.: 197). Self-absorption was prominent in the diary entries, although we know from other sources (letters to his sister, brother-in-law, and Theotokas) that Seferis was also concerned at this time with the political and economic crisis in his native Greece (a reflection of the international monetary crisis after the Depression in America). He also had thoughts about others, like his baby niece for whom he translated, in rhyming Greek, verses of D.H. Lawrence. His homesickness was expressed variously. For Theotokas' name day, he sent a card with the bust of Homer in the British Museum, and in "Letter to a Foreign Friend" (*On the Greek Style*: 165-166) he relates how he used to find temporary "shelter" in the aforesaid museum and the National Gallery:

> I remember the time— it now seems so long ago— when I was making my first faltering discovery of London, which I thought of as a gigantic seaport, and the English language, whose music sounded so much more fluid than that of our own tongue. Also, the shock I experienced at the sour taste of death in the fog, and the intensified circulation of fear in the arteries of the great city... I carried with me a great nostalgia, which was awakened on many occasions by the kind of formless sensitivity and patient, really cold politeness with which I was surrounded. I had no friends in England then. My only acquaintances were the crowds in the streets and the museums... I often had to rush out of my house to see again a fragment of the Greek marbles... or a small portrait by El Greco at the National Gallery.

When Seferis left England in February, 1934, he could not foresee the circumstances under which he was to set foot in that country again. It was 10 years later and during the last worst air raids on London that Seferis accompanied a Greek politician on an official mission to England, flying there from Cairo via Morocco. It was a very difficult time for him, for apart from the general uncertainty of the political situation and the troubles of exile, Seferis felt victimized by his own people, an object of intrigues and petty jealousies. The book he read during the flight was characteristic of his feelings at the time, Kafka's *The Castle*, "a book that reflects well enough," he noted on the margin, "my present situation: this man who tries to enter an impenetrable castle, high on the hill, and becomes entangled, every time, in endless nets... like a fish out of the water" (July 14, 1944) (*Meres D*: 334).

When the plane finally landed in England (Swinton), the greenness of the landscape impressed Seferis just as it had impressed him in 1931: "I think I remember these houses with their thatched roofs and the small quiet windows, and all that green colour which I missed so much in Egypt and which my eyes absorb now, like water. I think I have strolled about here ten or twelve years ago." And a little later, he wrote, "Fields of England, strange workings of memory. In the last ten years I have not recalled them more than four or five times, remotely, abstractly. Now, it is as though I left them asleep, like that, last Sunday" (July 15, 1944).

Two weeks later, Seferis was a guest at the country estate of David Wallace, an English officer with whom he had worked in Greece and Egypt.

> In the afternoon, we took a walk on the green hills and through wooded paths. Many aeroplanes in the sky. Only those remind you of the war. We had supper at Beechwood [one of the houses on the estate]. Good wines. Nine rooms, remnants of a time when they hosted twenty or thirty people during weekends. When we went upstairs to sleep, the servant had emptied our poor little suitcases and arranged everything neatly. Through the window, I could see sheep ruminating calmly, almost at the same level with where I sat in the armchair. Slow and quiet end of the day, that darkening which seems never ending at this time in England. The room which they gave us is entirely painted in white and lead colors. Pictures of plants all around the walls: *Calanthe Vestita, Oncidium Sarcodes, Cymbidium Eburneum*. I feel sleep pressing on my eyelids as I take these names down...
> (July 24, 1944)

The man who used to copy in his notebook the exotic names of plants that he had found in the parks of London during the peaceful years of 1931-34 still did so, during the critical days of 1944. He had a sensual feeling for language, and the ruins of the war elicited a similar response from his eyes. His descriptions were frugal, but also sensitive: "As we were entering the park from Bayswater, across from a house that had been hit, the trees were bare, without a single leaf, as if you had skinned them with a knife" (July 19, 1944). In the many ruins around Saint Paul's, Seferis noted the violet flowers that grew where there used to be high buildings. He witnessed the evacuation of women and children from London because of the "robots." In the 1930s Seferis had recorded in his diary fleeting impressions from the anonymous, often miserable crowds that he saw in the streets of the English capital, the unemployed and the drunk. In his brief 1944 visit, he felt deep sympathy for all of those, regardless of their social status, who were paying a big price for the war, above all the old and the very young whom he saw sleeping in the subway stations (scenes immortalized in the drawings of Henry Moore):

> In the tube. Wooden scaffolds filled with people. Others are lying on the pavement. Your eyes stop on the faces of the old and the children; a little girl with blond hair, or tired, fixed eyes on heavily wrinkled faces. You would say that they are asleep like that, with eyelids open as if they were dead, while the trains come and go.
> (July 26, 1944)

In the early hours of July 19, Seferis was kept awake by the persistent bombings around the "Ritz," where he and his Greek companion were staying. By 2:20 a.m., he had counted six explosions and described the workings of an explosion as he caught them by ear. Exhausted, he fell asleep while the bombings went on. "One of the worst nights since the war began," the waiter who brought them breakfast said in the morning. Several days later, Seferis visited a Greek acquaintance at her estate in Frimley, where he saw and admired a huge, strong bull that (as they informed him) had been recently deprived of one of his five heifers, when a doodlebug killed her. Seferis could not miss recording the graphic detail.

But how concrete had the human landscape of England become for Seferis by 1944? Much more concrete. Seferis had not yet met T.S. Eliot, whom Seferis had translated and published in 1936 with copious notes, but, in his capacity as foreign press officer in the Greek Ministry of Press and Information since 1938, Seferis had the opportunity to work with several Englishmen. These contacts continued and even increased during the war years because of the common war effort between Greece and England. All these associations and their echoes, if any, in the poetry, as well as in the critical and confessional prose of Seferis, deserve separate treatment. Here, it may suffice to suggest Seferis' fair and independent mind vis-à-vis the British people he met and worked with during these years, by considering part of a 1944 entry in his diary, precisely from the period of his brief visit to England during the war that we have just been discussing:

> In the station, P. with his [Greek] shepherd's staff, waiting to travel to London. He is a fair-haired Scot, not quite thirty perhaps. Before the war, he used to make beer and whiskey. Now, he is a lieutenant-colonel and link with the resistance in the Peloponnese. He has learned Greek. He is going to see his wife for a few days, after two years. Should he phone her first, or not? This is his big question... [On the train] "England never changes. England is always Sleepy" [sic], P. says, as if he was singing his deeper yearning. Which yearning? That for his wife? For his adventures in Greece? His feelings about the destiny of the war? He is reading Tolstoy's *War and Peace*. We exchange bitter-sweet jokes about Greece. He observes: "I do not trust the Greeks who speak good English."— "You are right," I say, "I have the same feeling about the British who know our language well." An old breed they are, these young men (I mean the better ones, not the levantine kind) who begin their political career with adventures in our land. The type strikes me as half intellectual and half corsair of the Drake period. As an individual, you can't help liking them. It is another story that they have turned us upside down while being trained on how to crop the scanty hair on our poor heads. After all, however high their social status is, they pay like the others.
> (July 15, 1944)

Literature could not be very much in Seferis' mind during those critical days of 1944. However, four days before flying back to Cairo, Seferis records meeting Cyril Connolly in the lobby of the Ritz, without giving any other details, while several days earlier he had asked Leonard Russell, editor of the literary page of *The Sunday Times*, to name some of the better books that had appeared in England during the war period. "This is a difficult question," was Russell's only answer.

No poems of Seferis seem to have originated directly in the impressions of his month-long official visit in the England of 1944. But there is a poem from his Egypt days, "An Old Man on the River Bank," in which the image of the Nile seems to overlap with the vision of the Thames as Seferis saw it in the 1930s, as well as the motif of the river that he had found in Eliot's *Four Quartets*. In this poem, Seferis considers the fortuities of his life and the accidents of the war, the "hungry children and the chasm between" himself and his companions "and the companions calling from the opposite shore" (that is, from occupied Greece), the "bluish light" of the hospital and the "glimmer on the pillow of the youth" who had undergone surgery, all these implacable urgencies and fatalities. He feels that he should still go forward:

> [...] like
> the long river that emerges from the great lakes
>   enclosed deep in Africa,
> that was once a god and then became a road and a benefactor, a
>   judge and a delta;
> that is never the same, as the ancient wise men taught,
> and yet always remains the same body, the same bed, and the same
>   Sign, the same orientation.
> (lines 10-15)

The central river motif of the poem is further elaborated and brought into connection with the fluid yet persistent ways of the human psyche in the following passage:

> If pain is human we are not human beings merely to suffer
>   pain;
> that's why I think so much these days about the great river,
> that symbol which moves forward among herbs and
>   greenery
> and beasts that graze and drink, men who sow and harvest,
> great tombs even and small habitations of the dead.
> That current which goes its way and which is not so
>   different from the blood of men.
> (lines 20-25)

The year and a half that Seferis spent in England in 1951-1952 as a senior member of the Greek Embassy in Britain were not conducive to personal writing (even his diary entries were comparatively few), but brought contacts with English intellectuals, especially, at last, with Eliot. Judging from Seferis' *Meres F* (first 50 or 60 pages), we find certain similarities in mood and attitudes from this period and from his first extended stay in England in 1931-1934. His mystical attachment to the Greek landscape and traditions was not overtly expressed, but was evident in his gentle but persistent suggestion that Eliot visit Greece. He even arranged for a luncheon between Eliot, Sir Charles Peake, the British ambassador to Greece at the time, and himself in order to promote the idea of the trip, which Eliot seemed to want, but ultimately was never able to attempt. Seferis also remembered the Greek poets Palamas and Sikelianos, the latter having died only recently. More and more insistently, he commented on the dichotomy between his personal creative impulses and his regimented professional life. Thus he commented to Eliot, who advised him not to evade his professional obligations because [more] freedom from such restrictions did not necessarily lead to more happiness or greater creativity. Seferis seems to have registered Eliot's view with approval. Perhaps it confirmed some notion that he himself already had about such matters.

We no longer hear much about loneliness. His wife Maro was now with him, and England was not the impersonal environment of his 1931-1934 years when he knew nobody. His reactions to the natural and human landscape of the country were few and brief, but usually connected with encounters he had with specific individuals. He and his wife seem to have enjoyed a visit to Cambridge in June, 1951, around convocation time, during a sunny day when, as Seferis put it, "the banners of the colleges added good cheer to the blue sky, reminding me of the kites we used to fly in Smyrna on Clean Monday [the first Monday of Lent]" (*Meres F*: 22). The visit to Cambridge included a meeting, his first, with E.M. Forster and George Savidis (then a student at Cambridge)— the latter was eventually to become the main editor of Seferis' works in Greece. Seferis admired Forster as a great liberal thinker (he had similar feelings for André Gide, for example), but both Seferis and Savidis undoubtedly appreciated Forster's early interest in the work of the Greek poet Cavafy and his efforts to promote this work in England. Cavafy seems indeed to have been the main topic of conversation in this first meeting with Forster (*Meres F*: 22-23).

Seferis appears to have enjoyed less a ceremonial gathering of people at the Buckingham Palace gardens one month later; he found the party a rather bland affair, an event that for him marked Britain's post-war adaptation to new circumstances. But Seferis felt uncomfortable among large crowds anyway. He most enjoyed being with select friends as when, for example, during an excursion to White Horse, Berkshire, he was photographed smiling (a rare thing with him) with the also smiling Maro, the Greek painter Ghika, and the English writers John Betjeman and Osbert Lancaster (the latter was better known as a humorist and cartoonist). The picture, taken with Seferis' own camera, illustrates *Meres F*, as does another from Haseley Court Park: a scene with shrubs shaped like chess pieces and with a sundial whose Greek motto Seferis transcribed in his diary. The notations of the visit are brief, almost telegraphic. Seferis probably never had the opportunity to rework them into a normal entry as he had been planning.

More interesting, though also succinct, are Seferis' word sketches of certain interiors: the "Petit Club Français," situated on an "almost apocryphal" side street off Saint James, in London, a "moth-eaten dollhouse, with dim lights and threadbare carpets on the stairs." The occasion is a cocktail party given by Louis MacNeice, during which Seferis met Eliot for the second time (*Meres F*: 30-33). On another occasion the Seferises dined with the Warners and the Connollys in a stately old house, in an attic room "under the big rafters of the ceiling, the room where [the painter] Constable had died" (*Meres F*: 41). Naturally Seferis wanted to describe Eliot's small, cell-like office near Russell Square when he went to see and say goodbye to Eliot in October, 1952, shortly before he had to leave Britain for an ambassadorial post in Beirut. He took the bus from home and then walked through districts that he had associated, 20 years earlier, with Thomas de Quincey's *Confessions of an Opium Eater*. He had first gone there to buy books by Eliot. Now he found the building where Eliot had his office standing intact in its corner among the ruins of the blitz bombings. Later, his conversation with Eliot brought back memories from the 1944 visit to London and the crowd scenes in the subway stations (*Meres F*: 48-49).

Meres F offers glimpses into other social and cultural activities of Seferis during this time: music concerts that he attended and briefly described, a ballet performance, a professional trip to Belgium to represent Greek poets at a symposium, a reading of his poetry on the BBC with the help of Louis MacNeice and Rex Warner (his translator), a visit with MacNeice to a pub where he met Dylan Thomas.

Finding it difficult to concentrate on his own writing, Seferis copied (presumably with revisions) his early unfinished novel, which was posthumously published with the title *Six Nights on the Acropolis*. He needed to re-establish some rapport with his past. On the other hand, his mind remained observant and open to new associations, as the following entry from August, 1951, suggests:

> Among the envelopes I open and check in the morning I notice one from the London County Council: a small margin printed in green, on the left corner, includes [Spenser's] *Sweet Thames! run softly; till I end my song*, under it [the words are in block letters]: Royal Festival Hall. I wonder, would they have advertised this line without the precedent of *The Waste Land* [where Eliot also quotes the line]? Whatever they may say, sooner or later, even the most difficult poetry becomes a common possession, a public taste, at the end. I had already noticed that in my student years, one evening at the Casino de Paris: within an ordinary musical revue there was a most spectacular scene, a blend of satanism, religiosity and sensualism, pure *Fleurs du mal*.
>
> The other day, while I was walking to my office, I was stopped by a middle-aged woman who stuck into my hand a small printout. Title: "The Cup."— It started like that: "It is the topic of conversation in thousands of homes, offices, and workshops... What is the secret of its absorbing interest? It is just that the English Football Association Cup stands for an achievement— a goal reached (in more sense than one)"; and a few lines later, this is associated with the gospel (Matt. 26: 42): "Father, if this cup may not pass away from me, except I drink it, thy will be done."
>
> When I wrote about the football in that letter on Eliot, I couldn't

imagine I was so close to the truth. The young Cyril who shouts "crumpets" in the church, does the same in the reverse.[21]

Seferis was a reserved and often self-conscious man, one who "se voyait voir"— to remember Valéry's *La soirée avec Monsieur Teste*, which Seferis translated into Greek. But he was also a man with a sensual feeling for his surroundings, both natural and man-made, including art. George Braque has written that it is not enough for an artist to make the others see what he paints, he must make them feel it as well.[22] Seferis quoted this statement of Braque with obvious approval, while commenting on the work of the Cypriot painter Diamantis.[23] For Seferis the aesthetic was an extension of the sensual. We thus understand his impulsive visits to the London museums to look at his favorite exhibits and the ways in which he tried to salvage from the English landscape whatever could compensate for his being away from Greece. Loner though he was, he needed human companionship, and he missed this during his first stay in England. Again, the substitute was found in the arts, music that Seferis heard with great concentration, poetry that he wrote with even greater attention, eventually with encouragement from Eliot's work. The England-based Seferis of 1931-34, of July-August 1944, and of 1951-52, was a Greek poet, conscious of his heritage and eager to honour and continue the literary tradition of his land. He was also ready to learn from other places, other traditions, and creatively to "steal" from other contemporary writers. He remained true to his belief, variously expressed in his essays, that there was no parthenogenesis in art. In patent or latent ways, creation was ultimately a collective business.

NOTES

1. Two of the readers of this chapter (as it was first published in the *Journal of Modern Greek Studies*) have made interesting comments on this point. Peter Levi remembers that there is a type of natural fog in Greece that seamen call *poussi* and that the pre-1950 London with its smog is similar to the smoggy Athens of today. George L. Huxley notes that Seferis' experience in England helped contrast the clarity of Attica, as it was then (1931-34), with the fog of London at that same period, while today we have a reversal of air in the two areas.

2. Here the Greek word *diskos* carries its double meaning, "phonograph record" and "serving tray."

3. Cf. with what Seferis wrote to his sister Ioanna (Tsatsos 1982: 203): "But I so long for Attica. The pines and the sea. These two things are before my eyes every day, like mythological creatures, in their changing aspects always new. A man must be away from his country at a mature age if he is to understand the *Odyssey*."

4. Allusion to E.A. Pope's *A Narrative of A. Gordon Pym*, from the tenth chapter of which Seferis had borrowed the epigraph of his poem "The Mood of a Day" (*Turning Point*).

5. Cf. with Chapter Three, p. 85.

6. Both Vayenas: 198-200, and *passim*; and D. Maronitis: 97-107, have commented extensively and perceptively on "Hampstead," especially in contrast to the poem by Angelos Sikelianos, "Thalero."

7. In R. Beaton's "Life at Close Range," review of *Meres B*, in *Times Literary Supplement*, September 17, 1976.

8. Harvard University Press, 1970. Seferis' introduction to this book may have been a partial compensation to Harvard for his refusal to deliver a similar lecture series at Harvard in 1969. See Introduction, p. 19.

9. The last simile may be likened with another involving El Greco. Under December 20, 1931, Seferis wrote: "The other day I found an old note of mine: 'National Gallery, 1924: A brush-stroke of Theotokopoulos [El Greco] like a Cretan fifteen-syllable line.'" This simile, which was not in fact made by Seferis but by a friend of his, is clarified in Seferis' *On the Greek Style*. 94-95.

10. A similar turn of phrase was used, many years later, by the Greek writer Nikos Gabriel Pentzikis, in reference to Seferis' pessimism, against which Pentzikis proposed the alternative of Christian faith. Seferis, according to Pentzikis, does not dare to get up and dance off his worries. His ego is too strong for that. "And yet, the whole thing is no more complicated than an inoculation" (in "Essoteriki Katathesis peri tou Piitou Yeoryiou Seferi," G. Savidis, ed., *Ya to Seferi*: 152-154).

11. See, in general, John E. Rexine, "The Diaries of George Seferis as a Revelation of his Art," *World Literature Today*, 61, 2 (1987), 220-223.

12. A listing of parallels in the essays of Eliot and Seferis is provided by A. Nakas (1978). See also Nakas' essay on Eliot in *I Lexi*, 43 (1985), 271-276.

13. Cf. the relevant passage in Part IV of the poem (in *Turning Point*):

Two serpents, beautiful, apart, tentacles of separation
crawl and search, in the night of the trees,
for a secret love in hidden bowers;
sleepless they search, they neither drink nor eat.

Circling, twisting their insatiable intent
spins, multiplies, turns, spreads rings on the body
which the laws of the starry dome silently govern,
stirring its hot, irrepressible frenzy.

14. *Sic* in the original, after "I read."
15. Cf. with "Seferis and the 'Mythical Method,'" in Keeley: 68-94.
16. See here, p. 48.
17. In fact, the column, whose drums are still strewn on the ground where they fell, was a casualty of a violent windstorm in 1852. Several Greek poets wrote poems on the fallen column.
18. The 1940 edition of *Book of Exercises* and subsequent editions of Seferis' poetry did not include the poems for Tuesday and Wednesday, which had been lost and found again in the 1960s. These were first published in Italy, and are now included in the expanded *Seferis* by Keeley-Sherrard.
19. The Greek *arkito vios* (enough of life) are the words that Cassandra speaks last (in Aeschylus, *Agamemnon*, 1324), before she enters the palace at Mycenae to die.
20. *On the Greek Style*: 69: "We went out into the empty streets of the becalmed city. On the wet pavement we could see, painted in multicolor crayons, the figure of Christ, with a discolored crimson forehead and heart..."
21. See T.S. Eliot, *Coriolan, I*, "Triumphal March": 42-45.
22. In *Le jour et la nuit, Cahiers 1917-52* (Paris: Gallimard, 1952).
23. In Seferis-Diamantis: 16.

Chapter Three
DWELLERS IN THE GREEK EYE: GEORGE SEFERIS AND LAWRENCE DURRELL

"All my favourite characters have been/ Out of all pattern and proportion," Lawrence Durrell announces at the start of his poem "Mythology" (*Collected Poems*: 251)[1] which he once sent to Seferis, primarily to amuse him. Seferis became sufficiently interested in the poem to translate it into idiomatic Greek appropriate to the style of the original (*Andigrafes*: 133). Durrell's claim to have a predilection for extraordinary characters is certainly true of his fictional characters, especially those of the *Alexandria Quartet*, the work that made him famous. It was also true of some real characters whom he had known, either personally, like George Katsimbalis, Miller's *Colossus of Maroussi*, who figures in "Mythology," or Cavafy, the Alexandrian poet whom he knew through his work. To some degree, Durrell's assertion may also be taken to include himself as well as Seferis.

The two men, the extroverted Durrell and the introverted Seferis (senior to Durrell by twelve years) were close friends through most of Seferis' life and sources of inspiration for each other, particularly during the early part of their acquaintance. The Cyprus conflict eventually found them in different camps and may have soured their friendship (judging from Seferis' diaries and correspondence), but the break seems to have been temporary. Through the 1960s they kept in touch and exchanged letters, though less frequently than in earlier years. They also wrote brief memoirs about each other. Durrell's on Seferis post-dates the latter's death in 1971.

In his memoir on Durrell (originally published in French),[2] Seferis turned to the war period when he, Durrell, and several other writers, English and Greek, were self-exiles in Egypt, and to Durrell's poems on Greek themes. Seferis had received about 20 letters from Durrell during the wartime period. Some of these were written, in the words of Seferis, "on anything that came to hand," some "decorated in the margins with multicolored drawings," some with "the sender's profile quickly sketched in place of the signature, like an ideogram." Seferis used two of these letters in his memoir. The first letter dated from around the end of April or beginning of May, 1941, and the second from around October, 1943.[3] The letter from 1941 is short, almost telegraphic in its urgency. Durrell and his family (first wife Nancy and baby daughter Penelope, or "Pinkie") had to be evacuated to Egypt from Crete, and Seferis— also in Crete but destined himself to leave the island very soon, although he did not know this at the time— was asked to take care of Durrell's luggage when it arrived by ship from Kalamata, Greece. Seferis was never able to do that, and the luggage was lost or captured by the Germans. One result was the loss of several letters from Henry Miller to Durrell— the very opposite happened when Miller lost several of Durrell's letters to him from the period 1941-1943 while travelling around America, studying the habits and mores of what he called *Homo Americanus*. In a letter of Seferis to Miller, dated December 15, 1941, we read about Seferis' and Durrell's time on Crete:

> I love Larry, he's got wonderful moments. I remember him in Crete. He came from Kalamata, on a sort of boat like the one you used to go to Spetses— with Nancy and Bouboulina.[4] We were starving when we met that night. Nancy waiting with her child for some food in a very sad hotel. Everything was full up in the town. The taverna stuffed with a queer crowd of soldiers and homeless civilians, sweeping the dishes like grasshoppers on a vineyard. After a tremendous struggle we succeeded in getting some cold rice, and left without paying, because the waiters were drowned in the compactness of this mad crowd. We parted in the blacked-out narrow street, under the extraordinary clusters of the sky. After one or two days he was gone to Egypt.[5]

The 1943 letter of Durrell to Seferis, printed in Seferis' memoir on Durrell, discusses the poem "Mythology" mentioned earlier, and suggests that Durrell had already started the novel that later became *Justine*, the first part of his *Alexandria Quartet*. The commentary on "Mythology" reflects material that we also find in Seferis (*Meres D*: 283-285).

The three letters of Durrell to Seferis, now first published below, come from the periods 1940-1941 and 1944 and thus bracket, chronologically, the two letters published by Seferis in his memoir and a third, intermediate letter from Seferis to Durrell that has been printed (in *Meres D*: 159-160) and will be mentioned later. But before we discuss these letters and other material from the war and later years as illustrations of the relationship between Seferis and Durrell, we should describe its background.

II

In 1935 all the Durrells, the widowed mother and four children aged 10 to 23 (Lawrence was the oldest and Gerald the youngest), moved to Corfu, Greece, from England in search of an agreeable climate and inexpensive life. The background of this eccentric move and many picturesque details of the Durrells' sojourn in Corfu are given in two books by Gerald Durrell, *My Family and Other Animals* (first published in 1957) and *Birds, Beasts and Relatives* (1969), and in Lawrence Durrell's more poetic but equally personal *Prospero's Cell* (1945). Lawrence had written and published poetry, but his main ambition was to be a best-selling novelist. His first two books in prose, *Pied Piper of Lovers* and *Panic Spring*, were neither commercially nor critically successful. He wrote his third book, *The Black Book*, under the liberating influence of Henry Miller's *Tropic of Cancer*. Durrell had written a fan letter to Miller and this started a long and rich correspondence between the two. In *Blue Thirst* (17), Durrell says that he was virtually bombarded by Miller (who was then living in Paris) with "a great deal of encouragement and documentation and masses of ideas." In *Prospero's Cell* (22), we hear of Miller's "rambling exuberant letters from Paris" being received in Corfu and read to the delight of Durrell's friends, who included the Armenian writer Zarian, the Anglo-Greek physician and encyclopedic "monster" Theodore Stephanides, and others. Durrell finally met Miller in Paris, in September of 1937, and decided to have *The Black Book* brought out by the Obelisk Press, which had also published Miller's books. Durrell's publishers, Faber and Faber (where Eliot had been very helpful), were prepared to publish the book themselves but with cuts that Durrell disliked.

In 1939 Miller visited Greece, as a first step in a long itinerary he was planning, with Tibet as the ultimate destination. Up to that point, he was not especially interested in the Mediterranean world, but he gradually became interested in Greece through Betty Ryan, a young lady who was living in the same building with him in Paris, and through the "poetic" letters he received from Durrell. Once in Greece, he was captivated by it. The outcome of his affair with that country and people was, of course, *The Colossus of Maroussi*, which he always considered to be his happiest book and which Durrell considers one of the two best books about Greece, the other being his own brother Gerald's *My Family and Other Animals*. Durrell appears several times in *The Colossus*. When war was breaking out in Europe, Durrell— Miller wrote— sought to enlist in the Greek Navy for service on the Albanian frontier, "because he thought more of the Greeks than he did of his own countrymen." We are also given a portrait of a different Durrell in Miller's description of a trip to Mycenae and Sparta, where Durrell's fussiness over an order of boiled eggs at some humble restaurant revealed to Miller "the Englishman in Durrell" and to himself his own "American" identity.

In "A Conversation with Seferis" (Keeley 1983: 198-199) we learn that Durrell was with Miller when they first met Seferis (via Katsimbalis who knew Theodore Stephanides) and that Seferis appreciated the fact that those two non-Greek writers seemed to understand his poetry much better than some of his Greek friends. The encounter is described more fully (in *Meres C*: 131-132):

> At Katsimbalis', in Maroussi, Henry Miller and Lawrence Durrell. I found them all in the dining room finishing their tea. George [Katsimbalis] had read them translations of my poems. So when I arrived I found an air of interest in me. I think that they (that is, Miller and Durrell) are the first English writers whom I have met. Durrell is a short and sturdy young man with the intelligent head of a satirist [...]. [He] told me that he was struck by the absence of sentimentalism in my poems (they are unsentimental in a good sense). This he found surprising in a Greek writer. He asked me whether I was brought up with English literature. He thought it odd that before the summer of 1931, as I pointed out, I had barely any contact with the English

writers [...]. At the end of the evening, Miller said to me: "What is peculiar about you is that you turn things inside out."

We recall that Seferis had first come upon the poetry of Eliot in 1931 and that up to that time his education had been overwhelmingly French. Durrell may have eventually understood that Seferis' unsentimentalism was, partly at least, due to Seferis' exposure to modern French writers like Valéry, Apollinaire, Laforgue, and Corbière.

In *Meres C* Seferis appeared to be impressed primarily by Miller, while he seemed to take Durrell for granted. This is understandable. A 48-year-old American like Miller, penniless but full of Dionysiac spirit, was more impressive than the much younger British expatriate Durrell, who had fallen out with his own people and was then searching for his identity in Greece, under what he called in *Prospero's Cell* the Greek "eye." Miller had to sail to America at the end of 1939. "For a long time," Durrell wrote in *The Greek Islands* (232), in reference to that period, "we had lived in the penumbra of a war declared on all sides but not implemented" in Greece, which technically was still a neutral country. "It was in the twilight of European history that I said goodbye to Henry Miller, who was ordered back to the States by his Consul."

The Durrells had already returned to Britain, except for Lawrence and his wife, who stayed on in Greece and moved to Athens from Corfu. There, Lawrence worked first for the British Embassy as a press officer and then for the British Council. He continued associating with men like George Katsimbalis, Seferis, Elytis, the painter Ghika, and others who were linked with the literary magazine *Nea Grammata* (New Letters), which was then ceasing its publication. He contributed to plans for a new magazine that this group hoped to use as a showcase for their work. Durrell wanted something really daring, something "in a smooth Dada way," that might secure for them a larger public. "What is important," he remarked, "is that poetry circulate, never mind the means." Seferis was skeptical. He thought that the lack of *kefi* (humour) in the Greek literary life of the time did not allow for such ventures (*Meres C*: 168).

On August 1, 1940, shortly before the Durrells were to move south to Kalamata, Seferis visited them at their home in Athens:

Last night at Larry's, in Psihiko. Their house is high on the hill, below the quarries. As soon as I entered, I felt that I had left Greece behind; I was at some suburb of London [...] the entrance hall with the exotic knives, the books on shelves, the drapes, the cheese after the fruit, and something beyond all these, an indefinable mood emanating from every piece of furniture, every fabric [...]. After dinner, Larry read us the first act from a drama on which he was working: the foreman, his wife, the convict, the prompter— he is planning a chorus of murderers. A terribly gloomy story, in the line of 16th century English drama.[6] Nancy (who I think can judge) finds it too *grand guignol*. I observed that the characters seemed to lack verisimilitude: their truth was not their own but the poet's. I also thought (but said nothing about this) that the English sometimes harbor inside them such a wild world— the civilized English as they usually call them. Consider only *Wuthering Heights*. Where else could a thirty year old girl have written such a thing?
(*Meres C*: 218).

As for Durrell's mood while in Athens, we have a poem, "Exile in Athens (1940)" (*Collected Poems*: 112), which is quite explicit. Durrell clearly misses the islands where he shared "a boundary with eagles," where he was "a subject of sails." In an earlier poem, "Finis" (*Collected Poems*: 25), the sea was cast as a mirror of the poet's pale thoughts: "There is a great heart-break in the evening sea;/ Remoteness in the sudden naked shafts/ of light that die, tremulous, quivering/ Into cool ripples of blue and silver.../ So it is with these songs." Later, the sea off the coast of Corfu made Durrell ecstatic rather than sadly contemplative. "Blue" became an obsessive word with him. It is used as a kind of magic stone in many of his poems and often surfaces in his letters: "We are dwellers in the Eye/ of Greece,/ dedicated to the service of this blue," Durrell wrote to Seferis in 1941 from Cairo.[7] But as "Exile in Athens" suggests, the blue could darken and become alien: "face/ Before the sea's blue negative,/ Washing against the night,/ Pushing against the doors,/ Earth's dark metaphors." Durrell idealized the countryside from the confines, the claustrophobia of the big city, the "stone city," as he calls Athens further on in the same poem (which reminds us of Seferis' remark about Durrell's house being near quarries).

III

The second half of 1940 found the Durrells at Kalamata, where Larry taught English. It is from there and in the excited atmosphere of the war— Greece had just been invaded by Mussolini's forces that were driven back deep into Albania— that Durrell wrote to Seferis on November 9:

> Institute of English Studies
> Kalamata
> 9 November 1940
>
> Dear George,
>
> Just a line to thank you for your note; at last we begin to see the star of Greece rise in all its splendour. I'd love to see Katsimbalis on his horse riding over the Albanian hills, and Tonio scouring the sea for the Italian Fleet. Great moments. By contrast we are in a tomb. These people are all paralysed with terror at losing their money and their lives and cringe about in shelters all day long. No parades, no celebrations— only an occasional air-raid alarm.
>   When I heard the news I telephoned Burn, asking [him] to close down the school but he thinks not; I have already applied for a liaison job with the British in Greece, but was informed that they are not doing anything worth mentioning! Still I'm waiting to hear. Perhaps naval intelligence could use me. I've just been reading *News of the "Week"* which we wanted to print ourselves last year! There is a wonderful letter in number II which begins "Englishmen! You are the ancient Greeks of modern times"! Send it to Henry [Miller]: he will like that. As for the Greeks— the spirit is wonderful! They deserve to enjoy their shattering victories in Albania, it seems as simple as eating cheese to them.

Here we have had many visitors but as yet no bombs, which is curious because Kalamata is quite important. The people are very wild and savage— the country people, I mean the Maniotes. They talk now of fighting Germany by themselves without help. We are living on the sea-coast in an awful house, and the bad weather is beginning. I have no *kephi* [that is, I am not in the mood] to write these days, unless it be a saga for Katsimbalis riding to battle or an ode to Churchill. The last speeches of Churchill, by the way, have been *great prose* as well as popular oratory. T.E. Lawrence once said: "When a man does a job that is bigger than he is, he grows to the size of it." That's rather what Churchill has done. As for Metaxas— Salut! O president of the Anglo-Hellenic league. He has become Barba-jani [that is, Uncle John] to the troops— with him and Tonio and you and Katsimbalis and Karageozi we do not need to worry. Between us we will make a new myth of Greece, and a new style of heart for Europe: and a *souvlaki* [that is, skewered meat] of the Eyetalians [sic].

Love from us all,

Larry

Tonio is the poet Antoniou, whom Durrell had met through Seferis, and Burn is A.R. Burn, the classicist and philhellene (and translator of Greek folk poetry into Scottish and vice versa), who was then in charge of the British Council's activities in Greece.[8] Metaxas was the Greek dictator Ioannis Metaxas, who, in the eyes of many Greeks, was redeemed from the abuses of his regime by not surrendering Greece to Mussolini in 1940. Durrell also uses "Karaghiozis" (in allusion to the popular shadow-theater hero) to represent the anonymous Greeks, mostly peasants, who, as soldiers, were successful in opposing the Italian invasion. Both here and in Seferis' translation of Durrell's "Mythology" (where, prompted by Durrell, Seferis rendered the poem's last line "Oh men of the Marmion class, sons of the free" by "O fitra tou megalou karaghiozi, yi ton eleftheron"),[9] Karaghiozis seems to be an equivalent of the "innocently crazy" and "spontaneously free", individual, who might be either a Greek soldier defending his country against overwhelmingly superior forces or a surrealist poet, like Ramon Gomez de la Serna, who had founded an association for the protection of inanimate objects. Seferis had remembered Ramon in his delirious talk after an anti-typhus injection and Durrell had been intrigued.

The letter also foreshadows a poem, "Letter to Seferis the Greek" (*Collected Poems*: 99-102) that Durrell must have written about this time— despite his disclaimer of being in the mood for writing serious verse. It was cast as a long letter in verse (16 stanzas of five to 13 lines each) to Seferis and shared in the euphoria that pervaded Greece in the period between the two invasions, the Italian and the German.

Here we have a paean or a hymn to victory that is also an elegy to the dead. The language is highly metaphorical. Some of the imagery has to be pondered, but the tone holds to a strong key and the reader is swept along from stanza to stanza. "Letter to Seferis the Greek" is moulded by the archetypal concepts of love betrayed, hubris, and nemesis, sin and remission of sin. Bankrupt Europe had to learn from the heroic resistance of a small nation, Greece, which, just as in the Persian invasions of the fifth century B.C., had acted against the gloomy predictions of the wise, "the calculations of the astronomers, the legends/ The past believed in could not happen..." We will not find a Greek equivalent of this poem in Seferis, where "ecstatic" moments are rare, but rather in Odysseus Elytis' *Heroic and Elegiac Song for the Lost Second Lieutenant of the Albanian Campaign* (1945).

The other Durrell letter to Seferis from this period, first published below, shows Durrell making efforts to improve his Greek:

Institute of English Studies
Kalamata
20 February 1941

Dear George,

It was good to hear from you and to know that I am here because I speak Greek: life is disposed to be ironic. But now the good weather has begun things are not too bad here: plenty to eat at any rate; only lack of good company is boring— and nothing to read. I suppose you couldn't gather up Henry's Greek book and post it to me: I would love to read it and would gladly pay postage whatever it may be: or better still, our Kalamata consul is now in Athens: his name is Kostopoulos and he would bring me the MS when he comes. You will see from the enclosed how famous I am getting as a modern Greek translator! If there's anything new you want "translated" according to my bastard method send Greek with *full English text*. Otherwise I can't do it! How about us doing *The Woman of Xante* [sic] together: you would do all the work and I would get the fame! I am sure Eliot would print it by Faber. Does the idea amuse you? I will try and find a Greek text here and we could do it by post. It's a good moment now! What do you say?

Love from us all.

Larry

[P.S.] Seriously let us collaborate on Solomos: you could write a critical introduction and appendix and I would help with the Englishing of the poem.

Henry's "Greek book" is of course *The Colossus of Maroussi*, as yet unpublished but in the hands of Seferis in manuscript form— long chunks of it, if not the entire work. It is not clear what Greek text Durrell had translated, taking the opportunity to deprecate himself as translator. The work which he proposes to Seferis for translation, *The Woman of Zaky[n]thos* by Dionysios Solomos, an incomplete narrative that the great poet left behind when he died, together with a number of unfinished poems, was, for Seferis, like the *Memoirs of General Makriyannis*, a model of the simple and honest style of writing. But it presents many problems of interpretation and leaves questions unanswered. For these reasons it is doubtful whether Faber and Faber would have ventured publishing it.[10]

IV

In Chapter VIII ("Epilogue in Alexandria") of *Prospero's Cell*, Durrell mentioned several of his fellow exiles in Egypt during the war, giving brief but expressive descriptions of Seferis and his wife: "Maro, the human and beautiful, in her struggle against apathy [...] the solemn face of Seferiades with its candour and purity." Early in this period, Seferis had to serve for several months in Pretoria, South Africa, before returning to Egypt in the Spring of 1942 to serve at the Greek Embassy in Cairo. While still in Pretoria, Seferis wrote to Durrell (in Cairo), enclosing in his letter the translation of a limerick he had written ("I think that limerick writing is a good exercise for lonely men, and suppose that the genre has been created in England because all of you are lonely like islands"), asking about Miller, whose *Colossus* he would have liked to translate into Greek. "I have all the feelings of a marooned man," Seferis added. "It is much better than not having feelings at all, as one of your distinguished essayists would have observed, I mean Thomas Stearn [Eliot]."[11]

While in Egypt, Durrell first supported himself and his family as a journalist, then served in Cairo as a press officer for the British Embassy, which subsequently sent him to Alexandria as an information officer. His wife took their daughter and moved to Palestine when there was fear of a German invasion in Egypt. The separation proved permanent. Durrell met another woman, a Greek-Jewish girl, Eve, whom he was to marry later. In 1943 Durrell was very active as a man of letters, editing, together with the writers Robin Fadden and Bernard Spencer, the magazine *Personal Landscape*, finishing his *Prospero's Cell*, publishing his first real collection of poems, *A Private Country*. During this time, Seferis was pouring out his frustrations through poems, like "Days of April '43" and "Actors, M.E. [Middle East]" (*Collected Poems*: 305, 511, 513) whose biting and darkly humorous style set them apart from his other, more introspective and solemn poetry.

Apart from his other activities, Durrell had been translating, with Bernard Spencer, poems of Seferis into English, intending to bring out a book as soon as it was completed. Durrell had been in fact drafted by Katsimbalis to do this job even before the outbreak of the war. Both of the following letters from Durrell to Seferis are about this project:

29 March 1944

Dear George,

Thank you for the corrections— we are having trouble in translating you so that you don't sound like Eliot— the technical similarities are quite as astonishing as the temperamental similarities.

    1. You are both "tentative" poets— not positive and dominated by an idea, but searching and feeling, a little faded and ridiculous: Prufrock and Pascalis.

    2. You both are after a statement of the unnameable thing and find it in a landscape. The rose-garden in Burnt Norton— Asini Acropolis.

    3. You both quote like hell.

    4. You are both elliptical.

    5. You both write bits of jazz and invent mythological characters. Eh bien quoi?

    [Lawrence Durrell]

The second letter is undated but seems to have come from the same period and was illustrated in a fashion similar to the other, with Durrell's "profile quickly sketched in place of the signature," as Seferis observed in discussing his correspondence with Durrell (pp. 77-78 above).

Dearest George,

Your little piece of autobiography is charming. I am glad to have teased you into doing it— of course I knew the facts: Have you forgotten that evening at Maroussi when Theodore, George, and I were battling with Pascalis— and the question of your common origin from the French symbolists together with Eliot was discussed by G[eorge Katsmbalis] with so much erudition? Perhaps you don't remember— at any rate we are forging ahead and will send you scripts a day or two hence. I want to hurry the book off so it doesn't conflict with the poems of all of us due to appear— the King of Asyny [sic] is a very great work, my dear— and it is lovely in English.

[Lawrence Durrell]

Durrell's comparative sketch of Seferis and Eliot is quite perceptive, but may have revived a ghost in the mind of Seferis. As early as 1933, Seferis had predicted that Greek critics would overplay his dependence on Eliot (*Meres C*: 118). In time, he grew touchy about the subject, especially after critics like Timos Malanos divided, rather too neatly, Seferis' development as poet between his early Valéryan period and his later Eliotic one. We do not know exactly how Seferis took Durrell's remarks that were obviously made in good faith— "Seferis is the Eliot of Greece," Durrell had also written in 1941 to Eliot's secretary Anne Ridler (*Spirit of Place*: 67)— but he may have tried to enlighten Durrell on Mathios Pascalis, one of several personae that Seferis had adopted in the writing of certain poems with the purpose of representing different sides of his personality. Durrell also wrote poems under the name Conon (*Collected Poems*: 127, 130).

The "evening at Maroussi" may have been the same occasion at which Seferis met Durrell and Miller in 1938, although we would expect a reference to Miller as well. The remark on the poem, "The King of Asine," last in Seferis' *Logbook I* poems (1940), foreshadows the title of Durrell's and Spencer's book of translations. *The King of Asine and Other Poems*, which was eventually completed with the collaboration of the Greek poet Nanos Valaoritis and published (with a preface by Rex Warner) as already mentioned, in 1948, by John Lehmann, after various delays that had to do with the instability in the lives of those involved with the project as much as with the shortage of paper in Britain right after the war.[12] In the papers of Seferis there is a brief letter to Seferis by Bernard Spencer in which we read: "If you like the translations, please give your consent *as soon as possible*, because Lehmann has got some paper— a rare thing in England (commoner in lavatories than in publishers' offices)."

In his memoir about Durrell, Seferis remembered Spencer, the prematurely deceased poet, whom he called "a beautiful soul/ like none that are made today" (quoting Laforgue). Spencer had joined the British Council in

1940 and was posted to Thessaloniki when Durrell was teaching at Kalamata. During the war he too was in Egypt and edited, as noted earlier, *Personal Landscape* with Durrell and Fadden. The magazine was published from 1942 to the end of the war, drawing on the work of several writers stranded in or posted to the Middle East. Spencer's first book of verse, *Aegean Islands* (1946), was highly thought of by Seferis (according to the recollection of Mrs. Maro Seferis). On the other hand, Kenneth Young (1950: 61) found Spencer's "more pictorial, less metaphysical" poetry lacking in comparison to the work of Durrell and Seferis, who probably influenced Spencer.

V

Durrell did not return to Greece, as Seferis did with the other members of his government, towards the end of 1944. He remained in Egypt until June, 1945, at which time he was appointed Press and Public Relations Officer for the Allied Government in the Dodecanese until March, 1947. *Reflections on a Marine Venus* (1953) recounts his experiences in Rhodes, and more broadly the Dodecanese, an area of the Greek archipelago that went through a transitional stage between its Italian occupation and its union with Greece in 1947. In the meantime, civil war had erupted in Greece, and Durrell remembered, in his memoir on Seferis, in the Tunisian magazine *Alif*, Seferis' bitter comment on these developments: "En 1918, après la Grande-Guerre, Dada s'est installé dans la littérature. Après cette guerre-ci, voilà Dada entré dans la vie politique!" The comment has tragic overtones that are very different from the playful connotations and Dadaist echoes of Durrell's "Mythology." As a diplomat and, particularly, as director for a time of the Regent's (Archbishop Damaskinos') political office, Seferis registered and felt to the marrow of his bones the Greek political troubles of the period. The poem he wrote in 1947, *Thrush*, is a mirror of his war experiences as much as a reflection of his attendant anxieties and an overwhelming desire for at least a spiritual transcendence.

Before returning to England, in 1947, Durrell called on Seferis, who invited Katsimbalis, the painter Ghika, and Rex Warner to gather around a phonograph record of Henry Miller's voice reading from his works. Miller had sent the record to Durrell, and he left it with Seferis. The publication of

The King of Asine and Other Poems in 1948 and the good reviews it had in Britain must have pleased both Seferis and Durrell. The latter was now in Argentina to work for the British Council, teaching English in the university town of Cordoba. But he did not stay there more than a year. He did not like South America much, although he found it somewhat better than North America which he had not visited yet! He longed for a post in Greece, but a suitable one could not be found; so he accepted the position of Press Attaché in the British Embassy at Belgrade and stayed there until 1952.

Durrell liked the landscape of Yugoslavia but was unable to meet and get to know the people on a human level, as he had done in Greece. In Communist Yugoslavia people were suspicious of each other, and the break between Stalin and Tito made the problem even worse. "The people are like moles," Durrell wrote to Henry Miller in the spring of 1950, "frightened to death, shifty, uneasy." (Durrell-Miller: 281). A writer who associated with Durrell was thrown into jail for falling under the influence of a western imperialist! But Durrell continued writing and his Yugoslavian experience resulted in the novel, *White Eagles over Serbia* (1957)— an adventure for young people— and *Esprit de Corps* (1957), a series of farcical short stories about Embassy life in the Balkans.

In his memoir on Seferis, in *Alif*, Durrell says that Seferis "was never overwhelmed by diplomatic life and took a wry and ironical view of it." The same holds true of Durrell, who dramatized the funny side of diplomacy not only in *Esprit de Corps*, but also in two other books, *Stiff Upper Lip: Life among the Diplomats* (1958) and *Sauve Qui Peut* (1966). The lecture "Propaganda and Impropaganda" (in *Blue Thirst*) is, similarly, a candid exposé of Durrell's repeated attempts at diplomacy during periods of crisis. The ephemeral and precarious world of politics, that Seferis had to endure for most of his adult years, and Durrell for various periods of his life, is contrasted— in Durrell's poem "Politics" (*Collected Poems*: 191)— with the subjective, indefinable, yet very real world of the poet.

When Durrell referred, in "Politics," to "The Englishman with his Apologizing Bag," he could not foresee that a few years later he would be playing such a role himself with his book on Cyprus, *Bitter Lemons*. It all began "poetically." In the fall of 1952, Durrell was still in Belgrade but ready for a move. "I'm quitting the service in December and we are setting off to Cyprus,

I think," he wrote to Miller. "No money. No prospects. A tent. A small car. I feel twenty years younger. Heaven knows how we'll keep alive, but I'm so excited, I can hardly wait to begin starving" (Durrell-Miller: 291).

VI

To earn money, Durrell got a teaching job at the Greek Gymnasium in Nicosia and settled in the Kyrenia district of the island after buying a Turkish house. On November 20, 1953, he wrote to Miller: "Night before last there was a bang on the front door and a shout and Seferiades walked in. You can imagine how warmly we embraced each other. He had not altered by a day, still the graceful and lovely humour— man and poet. He had never been to Cyprus before and is ravished by it." And in another letter, of January 5, 1954: "It was so lovely too to see Seferis again after so many years, as gentle and humorous as ever. I teach, you know, at the Greek Gymnasium, and he was brought down as a distinguished poet and given an oration, so I was able to be present as a master. He made a touching address to the boys full of thoughtful things very gently said." (Durrell-Miller: 298, 300). Seferis was Greek Ambassador at Beirut at the time, and though he had stopped over for two hours at the port of Limassol in December, 1952, on his way to Lebanon, he considered his 1953 visit to Cyprus to be his true first visit. During this visit he met several times with Durrell, Maurice Cardiff, Director of the British Council in Cyprus, and several Greek Cypriot educators, writers, and artists.

The conflict between Greece and Britain over Cyprus was growing at the time, but Durrell was still in the "neutral zone." Seferis was apprehensive that his private visit might become the object of political abuse. He had an opportunity to discuss developments with the Greek and British authorities, but on the whole the functions that various Cypriot cities organized in his honour had a broad cultural character. His diary notes from the period (*Meres F*) suggest the starting points of several of his *Logbook III* poems.

Several months later, Durrell accepted the position of Press and Information Director. According to the Cypriot painter Diamantis, in a letter he wrote to Seferis in August, 1954 (just before Seferis' second visit to the island) (Diamantis-Seferis 1985: 50), when Durrell asked Maurice Cardiff whether he should accept this position, he received the answer: "Do what you like but you will lose all your Greek friends." Cardiff thought, however, that something good might come out of Durrell's appointment to that sensitive post, since Durrell knew the Greeks so well. During his second visit to Cyprus, Seferis, who was again there for essentially private reasons, met Cardiff and learned that Durrell had become a nationalist after his service in Yugoslavia. He now trusted the official policy of the British Government. If Cyprus was thought to be indispensable to the Empire, so be it. "I remember," Seferis noted in his diary (*Meres F*: 147), "when he [Durrell] thumbed his nose against the English generals— and before that when he spoke ill of England, the time he was a pacifist." And in a letter to George Theotokas, dated December 28, 1954, Seferis made the comment, particularly sarcastic for an old friend, that he was afraid that Durrell was heading towards becoming a Subvice-Kipling! What annoyed Seferis above all was the attempt of British propaganda, that inevitably issued from Durrell's Office, to present Greek Cypriots as being not of Greek but of Phoenician origin.

The political situation worsened in 1955, with the start of the guerrilla war after the failure of the tripartite (England, Greece and Turkey) conference of London and the Turkish atrocities against the Greek community of Constantinople, and in 1956, after Archbishop Makarios was arrested and sent to exile. Durrell resigned his post and went to England where he wrote to Miller in October, 1956: "Cyprus is so tragic it doesn't bear talking about" (Durrell-Miller: 306). He wrote *Bitter Lemons*, his "apologia pro vita sua" in Cyprus, in a few weeks, and announced its publication to Miller in a letter from France, dated from February-March, 1957: "My book on Cyprus comes in September and will rustle a few dovecots, I hope" (Ibid.: 311). The book was very successful, both for literary and political reasons, and was awarded the Duff Cooper Memorial Prize. 1957 was, in general, a turning point in Durrell's career, for he was famous on both sides of the Atlantic soon after the publication of several of his books including *Justine*, the first part of his *Alexandria Quartet*. He settled in southern France, meaning to stay put, but still regretting the loss of his house on Cyprus. In January, 1958, he wrote to Miller: "I sympathise with you not wishing to voyage around. One's own house is such a step. Alas, I shall never get back to mine [in Cyprus] thanks to our fatuity and Turkish imbecility and Greek pottiness" (Ibid.: 328).

Whatever its biases, Durrell's *Bitter Lemons* is an open and honest account of its writer's Cypriot experience with its dilemmas and conflicting loyalties. Seferis distilled his own experiences of Cyprus in the poems of *Logbook III* (1955), dedicated "To the People of Cyprus, in Memory and Love." The collection has many facets and displays a variety of moods, from elation to a sense of doom and tragedy, from sorrow to affirmation, but it can also be seen as a resistance to the British attitude towards Cyprus, a resistance couched in figurative terms. The poem "Helen" (*Collected Poems*: 355-361) is a parable questioning the value of the sacrifices that *bona fide* people, Greek and non-Greek, made in the Second World War despite Britain's persisting post-war imperialism. Those who are addressed in "Salamis in Cyprus" (Ibid.: 383-389) as "Friends from the other war" are those honest fighters, some of them now dead, with whom the poet felt united in a common cause:

> Friends from the other war,
> on this deserted and cloudy beach
> I think of you as the day turns—
> those who fell fighting and those who fell
>   years after the battle,
> those who saw dawn through the mist of death
> or, in wild solitude under the stars,
> felt upon them the huge dark eyes
> of total disaster;
> and those again who prayed
>
> when flaming steel sawed the ships:
> "Lord, help us to keep in mind
> the causes of this slaughter:
> greed, dishonesty, selfishness,
> the desiccation of love;
> Lord, help us to root these out..."

The quoted prayer echoes, as the poet has informed us in a note, the wartime prayer of a British Commander, Lord Hugh Beresford, R.N., who fell in the battle of Crete. The poem ends in a dialogue, where the one speaker is the poet and the other may be an English friend like Durrell or Maurice Cardiff, or perhaps a quiescent part of the poet himself:

> — Now, on this pebbled beach, it's better to forget;
> talking doesn't do any good;
> who can change the attitude of those with power?
> Who can make himself heard?
> Each dreams separately without hearing anyone else's nightmare.
>
> — True. But the messenger moves swiftly,
> and however long his journey, he'll bring
> to those who tried to shackle the Hellespont
> the terrible news from Salamis.
>
> Voice of the Lord upon the waters.
> There is an island.
>
> *Salamis, Cyprus, November, 1953*

A forewarning that hubris led inevitably to tragedy and that the island of Cyprus would make its stand.

The inability of the British to assimilate the island into their own world, or fuse themselves with it, was sketched in light satirical terms in the rhyming poem "In the Kyrenia District," where the "cynic and philhellene" poet mentioned may have been Durrell. One of the two ladies chatting in the poem confessed not to feel entirely at home in Cyprus:

> — ah, this view
> that questions and questions. Have you ever
> noticed how the mirror sometimes
> makes our faces death-like? Or how that
> thief the sun
> takes our make-up off each morning? I'd prefer

the sun's warmth without the sun; I'd look for
a sea that doesn't strip one bare: a voiceless blue
without that ill-bred daily interrogation.

The silent caress of the mist in the tassels of
    dream would refresh me
this world isn't ours, it's Homer's—
that's the best description I've heard of this place.

It is significant that the poem ended with a reference to some Englishman called Bill (probably to be identified with the fallen commander of "Salamis in Cyprus") who died in Crete. The casual reference to this man in the middle of an idle chat (that wove together details pertaining to Britain as well as to Cyprus and was interrupted, at some point, by a dog called "Rex"),[13] was bitterly ironic of course: the supreme sacrifice that English soldiers made in a cause that united Greece and Britain during the Second World War had now lost its meaning and value in its British masters' cynical, and at best touristic, view of Cyprus. Durrell's synopsis of his Cypriot experience was, by analogy, given in his poem "Bitter Lemons" (*Collected Poems*: 238) which one could see as a prologue or epilogue to his book of the same title.

VII

In 1960, by the time the Cyprus issue was resolved with the signing of a treaty between Britain, Greece, and Turkey, Durrell had settled permanently in the Midi of France with his third wife, Claude, whom he had originally met in Cyprus. In 1962 he traveled to Israel and Greece on a journalistic assignment. On September 24, 1962, he wrote to Diana Menuhim (formerly Diana Gould) (*Spirit of Place*: 153-154):

> As you can imagine the Greek visit was most exciting, though Israel was interesting and rather moving, and I hope to write something about it. But Athens gave me back at a blow all my old friends whose touching warmth was really like a home-coming; made it like one I mean. We did a swift autumn tour of the Peloponnesus— deserted,

bare and blue! Dug out old taverns, discovered new. Above all had Katsimbalis and Seferis to ourselves for *days* on end. Such shouts, such gales of laughter, such memories exchanged! It was like a gasp of rare air and I felt twenty years younger.

In 1964 and 1967 there were reunions at Corfu where much had changed from the pre-war days.

In 1966, when Alan G. Thomas was planning *Spirit of Place*, he wrote to Seferis with the request that Seferis lend him, for use in the book, some of Durrell's letters to him. Thomas' letter lies among the papers of Seferis with a handwritten comment by Seferis that he had written to Durrell about the matter. "There are no Durrell-to-Seferis letters in *Spirit of Place*," which probably means that Seferis' response to that request was negative— not surprisingly, since Seferis rarely allowed any of his private letters to others or such letters to himself to be published while he was alive. He only made moderate use of such letters in his own writing, as we have seen in discussing his memoir about Durrell.

In 1972, a few months after the death of Seferis, Durrell wrote an obituary poem:

Seferis

Time quietly compiling us like sheaves
Turns round one day, beckons the special few,
With one bird singing somewhere in the leaves,
Someone like K. or somebody like you,
Free-falling target for the envious thrust,
So tilting into darkness go we must.

Thus the fading writer signing off
Sees in the vast perspectives of dispersal
His words float off like tiny seeds,
Wind-borne or bird-distributed notes,

To the very end of loves without rehearsal,
The stinging image riper than his deeds.

Yours must have set out like ancient
Colonists, from Delos or from Rhodes,
To dare the sun-gods, found great entrepots,
Naples or Rio, far from man's known abodes,
To confer the quaint Grecian script on other men;
A new Greek fire ignited by your pen.

How marvellous to have done it and then left
It in the lost property office of the loving mind,
The secret whisper those who listen find
You show us all the way the great ones went,
In silences becalmed, so well they knew
That even to die is somehow to invent.

(*Collected Poems* 321)

The poem is rhyming and thus approximates better a traditional funerary encomium or elegy. Seferis is portrayed as a sower of words that will invigorate those who listen to them. He is also a worthy promoter of Greek traditions and a man whose silences are as pregnant with meaning as his words. Seferis' supreme silence, that is, his death, is as eloquent as his life and work. This reminds us not only of Durrell's own "tears hushed" of the poem "Bitter Lemons," but also, and above all, of Seferis' work: the poem "Last Stop," for example (*Collected Poems*: 309-315), where Seferis' mind is with the anonymous heroes who "walk in the dark," or Seferis' comment on the poetry of Bernard Spencer, at the end of his memoir about Durrell, including verses of Spencer: "Separated, young lovers hold hands through letters/ Between them the world is a factory of fear. We admit/ That it is better not to admit the reason why..." Spencer had read him those verses but nothing had changed. The factory of fear was still there, "either in front of the stage lights or waiting in the wings." In fact there is an echo of Spencer's lines in Seferis' "Last Stop," when we read: "And if I talk to you in fables and parables/ It's because it's more gentle for you that way; and horror/ Really can't be talked about because it's alive,/ because it's mute and goes on growing."

Although Seferis did not find it natural to write heroic poetry, he had a passionate but painful attachment to Greece. As we shall see later, Miller called Seferis a "patriot" in allusion to that peculiar attachment that Miller felt he could not have for his own native land. But in the end, America proved large enough to accommodate even the disgruntled Miller. He settled and lived in California for the rest of his life. Durrell, who had a "simple, old-fashioned, perhaps slightly prickly British patriotism, his Kipling side," as G.S. Frazer put it in his essay on Durrell (*The Writers and their Work*: 26), also compromised by settling somewhere between England and the Mediterranean, an area that he recognized as his true spiritual center. But Seferis could not escape Greece, even though he had written, "Wherever I travel Greece wounds me." ("In the Manner of G.S.," *Collected Poems*: 197). He was an expatriate, like the other men, alienated from his own people and, judging from his diaries and indirectly from his poetry, often very unhappy in his professional career. Yet he belonged in the Greek landscape and always explored its emblematic meanings. The freedom with which Durrell moved for so many years from private to public life and vice versa is quite remarkable. Seferis saw the futility of leaving his job as a diplomat; he had earlier recognized the need for a "breastplate," however heavy that might be (cf., *Meres A*: 11: "It would be horrible if I were unable to pass my examination. My position is intolerable. As long as I do not have a surface or a cuirass, I cannot do anything [...].").

In any case, opposites do attract each other, and the freer temperament of Durrell must have initially attracted the reserved Seferis. He saw in the first of the two letters from Durrell that he discusses in his memoir on Durrell a "faith in happiness, a mystique of happiness" that Miller also seemed to embody. Seferis, who, as his fellow Greek Nikos Gabriel Pentzikis has written,[14] found it difficult to get up and dance off his worries, so to speak, seemed to be both fascinated by, but also mistrustful of his opposites, that is, men who overreacted to things. Above all he appreciated genuineness. He recognized, for example, the poet Sikelianos as a giant of sorts, but also felt that Sikelianos could be carried away. He disliked the rhetoricism of Kazantzakis and wondered whether his *Odyssey* was real poetry, while Durrell thought that, in Greece, Kazantzakis was someone whose work could be compared with his own. To an interviewer's question on modern writers with whom he found himself most naturally in sympathy he replied: "In France, with Montherlant and Proust; in America with Henry Miller; in Greece with Kazantzakis; in Argentina with Borges; in Italy with Svevo" (*Labrys*, 5: 42).

Miller and Durrell exchanged many accolades through the years. Miller was very old and half-blind in the late 1970s when they asked him to contribute a statement about Durrell for the special issue of *Labrys* referred to earlier, but he did not mince his words. He wrote that he considered Durrell to be "the finest writer in the English language today." Seferis liked the poetry of Durrell, but confessed not to be very fond of his fiction. He wrote in his memoir on Durrell, "Novels do not mean a lot to me, and I never gave much importance to the civil servant whose diplomatic buffoonery has made numerous people laugh in the chancelleries." He does not say why he did not like Durrell's novels, but perhaps he agreed with several English critics who found them overwritten, too rich and gaudy. Again, it should be pointed out that both Kazantzakis and Durrell were better accepted in America, which was still going through its epic period, than in England where nuance and understatement were valued more than vigour and directness of expression.

The meeting ground of Seferis and Durrell (whatever their affinities or differences of character) was of course Greece, in a real and also imaginative sense. In his memoir on Durrell, Seferis starts with Durrell's calling Greece (at the end of *Prospero's Cell*), "not a country but a living eye," an eye that records and measures the traveller, and recalls the riddle of the Theban Sphinx to which there was only one answer: *Man*. Seferis quoted the story with the Sphinx also in his Nobel acceptance speech in 1963 and described, in his diaries and essays, the Greek landscape as a landscape made in the measure of man. And it is Durrell's Greek poems that he discusses in his memoir.[15]

Durrell was inspired in several poems, as we have seen, by the work of Seferis, but Seferis never dedicated a poem of his to Durrell— the only two non-Greeks who were "given" poems by Seferis were Henry Miller and Rex Warner; nor was there a Seferis poem that related directly to a work of Durrell.

But this does not mean that Seferis did not respond consciously or subconsciously to things that Durrell, the poet or travel-writer, produced. There were echoes or similarities of tone and imagery between the two poets. For example, when we read "And those who abandoned the stadium to take up arms/ struck the obstinate marathon runner/ and he saw the track sail in blood,/ the world empty like the moon/ the gardens of victory wither: you seem in the sun, behind the sun," (Seferis *Thrush*, III) we may recall "those who went in all innocence,/ Whom the wheel disfigured: whom/ Charity will not revisit or repair./ The innocent who fell like apples" (Durrell's "Letter to Seferis the Greek").[16] The angle of vision was different in the two passages but there was a likeness of tone and a similar succession of images that lead to some still point, like a punctuation mark, that both finished and recapitulated dramatically what had been said.

It would be appropriate to finish this essay with the words of Durrell and Seferis on what particularly united them: the landscape of Greece.

From a letter from Durrell to Diana Gould (*Spirit of Place*: 82):

> Ah but Diana you should see the landscape of Greece— it would break your heart. It has such pure nude chastity; it doesn't ask for applause; the light seems to come off the heart of some Buddhistic blue stone or flower, always changing, but serene and pure and lotion-soft on the iris [...]. Lots of love and a bit of blue broken from the sky.

From Seferis (*Meres E*: 20):

> I sometimes think that the only thing that makes a difference between us and them [the English] (in thought, expression, architecture, language) is the light.

(Ibid.: 25):

> [In Greece] a ruined lintel with two or three leaves is really *something*. It is the light. The most insignificant objects toy and dance in the light and you observe their transubstantiation by it.

In conclusion, we may add that, with the Greek landscape and culture as mediators, Seferis and Durrell often shared thoughts and feelings that transcended their personal and national boundaries. The ways in which they described the light of Greece, for example, are idiosyncratic, but reflect a similar sensibility.

NOTES

1. Durrell had initially titled his poem "Mythology II" to distinguish it from "Mythology I," which he later changed to "Coptic Poem."
2. An English translation of the memoir was printed in the special issue on Durrell of *Labrys*, 5 (1979). I am quoting from, or referring to, this English translation here.
3. Durrell half-dated or did not date at all most of his letters. The problem was noted also by A.G. Thomas, in his preface to *Spirit of Place* (1969).
4. "Bouboulina," another name for Durrell's daughter "Pinkie." The name (of a well-known heroine of the Greek revolution of 1821) was also applied by Nikos Kazantzakis to lady Hortense of his *Zorba the Greek*.
5. I am quoting from the letter as it was printed in *Labrys* (note 2 above). Another slightly doctored version of this letter was published in Seferis (*Meres D.* 169-171).
6. In Durrell's *Collected Poems*: 80-81, we find "The Sermon, from a verse play," that most probably comes from the play mentioned by Seferis.
7. Quoted in a letter to Miller by Seferis (included in the *Labrys* issue, n. 2 above).
8. See also pp. 12-13 above.
9. Seferis explains his translation in *Meres D.* 283; in *Andigrafes*: 160; and in his memoir on Durrell (note 2 above).
10. *The Woman of Zaky[n]thos* can now be read in two different English translations: by Marianthe Colakis, in *The Charioteer*, 24-25 (1982-1983), 118-136; and by Peter Colaclides and Michael Green, in *Modern Greek Studies Yearbook*, 1 (1985), 153-171. The first translation is accompanied by the Greek original; both carry introductions and notes.
11. The letter, dated from the beginning of November, 1941, is printed in the Appendix for 1941 in Seferis (*Meres D.* 159-160, 160).
12. See p. 23 above. The book was preceded by Robert Levesque's *Seféris, Choix de Poèmes*, that was published in Athens in 1945. Levesque was another draftee of Katsimbalis and worked on his translations during the war with the assistance of Seferis' brother Angelos.
13. Cf. with pp. 31-32.

14. Cf. with note 10, p. 75, above. The relationship between Seferis and Pentzikis is explored in Thaniel: 128-130.
15. See also Peter Levi's "Lawrence Durrell's Greek Poems," in *Labrys* (note 2 above), 101-103.
16. See p. 85 above.

Chapter Four

A MEDITERRANEAN ENCOUNTER: GEORGE SEFERIS AND HENRY MILLER

In a letter dated May 6, 1972 (several months after the death of George Seferis in 1971), Henry Miller requested from Mrs. Seferis a Xeroxed copy of a diary on Greece that Miller had written in his own hand in a printer's "dummy" and given to Seferis as a gift, back in 1939 during Miller's first and only visit to Greece. He wanted to have this work printed in book form. Maro Seferis obliged and Miller confirmed receipt of the copy on June 23, 1972, asking permission to have this work (which was, in fact, an earlier and shorter draft of his *The Colossus of Maroussi*) published, and promising to send to Mrs. Seferis a signed copy of his own memorial volume, *My Life and Times*. Almost a year later, on March 8, 1973, Miller wrote again to Mrs. Seferis, announcing the forthcoming publication of his Greek diary. He wanted to include a photo of Seferis; if possible, one from the 1939 period when the two met and/or a photo of Seferis and himself together should there be one. Maro Seferis wrote back that she could not find any of the photos that Miller had requested, but sent him, instead, some photos of Seferis from later years. In the meantime, the diary had been published with the title *First Impressions of Greece*, and Miller sent Mrs. Seferis three copies. "The 'dedicaces' are in the back of the book," he added in his accompanying letter of June 14, 1973. "Those copies were leather bound especially for you." Miller was at the time 81 and ailing and wished to see everything he had ever written in print.

The publication of his Greek diary must also have been an exercise in nostalgia for Miller. His five month stay in Greece in 1939, after many years of hardship in France, had been a happy one. He was reminded of that visit, and of the manuscript that he had given to Seferis at that time, by the latter's interview with E. Keeley, now in "A Conversation with Seferis" (Keeley: 180-217). Keeley asked Seferis what had been his impressions of Henry Miller when they first met in 1939, and Seferis replied:

I like Miller because he is a very good-hearted man, and I think—
excuse me for saying so, but this is not a criticism: it is great praise to
say about a writer that he is a good man— Miller has a great deal of
generosity in him. For example, when the moment came for him to
go back to America (He was advised to do so by the American consul.
As an American national, he had to return home because the war was
approaching.), he said to me one day: "My dear George, you've been
so kind to me, and I want to give you something." And he produced
a diary which he had been keeping during his stay in Greece. I said:
"Look here, Henry. But after all, I know that you are going to write
a book, and you can't write the book— I mean you might need your
notes." He said: "No. All those things are here," pointing to his head.
I offered to make a typescript copy for him. "No," he said, "a gift
must be whole." Well, that's a splendid way of behaving, I think. And
I shall never forget that. The diary was a sort of first draft of the
Colossus. But with more personal explosions. And more jokes, of
course.
(Ibid: 200)

It appears that Miller read Seferis' interview, when it was first printed in
The Paris Review, in 1970, and tried to re-establish contact with Seferis with
the following letter, dated February 16, 1971, and mailed from Pacific Palisades,
California:

Dear George:

I can't tell you how delighted I was to read the interview with you
given in the *Paris Review*. I don't mean the reference to myself (which
was a beautiful tribute) but the whole tone of your words— so like
you, so warm, so humble, so honest, so unpretentious— *and* spoken
like a true poet!

I can still hear your voice in my ears— after all these years. I
am sure it still remains the same. And how I envied you your

patriotism— rather, your love of Greece— something I have been never been able to feel for my own country.

I hope our dear Katsimbalis is not suffering too much. I heard he was laid up with some affliction. Why I don't write any of you I can't explain. But I do think of you often and of the wonderful reception you gave me. Seems as if it were only yesterday!

I read almost no contemporary poets, largely because I find them too abstract. I suppose I get my necessary dosage of poetry through the few prose-poets still alive.

I like so much, I repeat, the way you speak of the poet and poetry. You are so human, so understandable, so very wise. God bless you!

Since I do not have your address in Greece, I am sending this care of *Paris Review*— I hope it reaches you eventually. Perhaps I might have reached you, as one does Picasso— just G.S.— Greece. Or "Somewhere in the world."

Give my best to all my old friends, won't you please? And stay well— and write only when it pleases you. It's the only way.

Ever yours,
Henry Miller

Seferis drafted a reply to Miller's letter, which, as he said, had made him realize that good friendships grow old like good wines. He enlightened Miller on George Katsimbalis (the hero of *The Colossus of Maroussi*), who now had weak legs, and the poet Antoniou who had retired from his sea-captain's job but was in good health. As for himself, Seferis followed Miller's advice to write only when it pleased him. A final note was relevant to Miller's own interview for *The Paris Review* that Seferis had sought out and read. A transcription of perhaps this final item in the Seferis-Miller correspondence has been published, along with four other of Seferis' letters to Miller, by J. Stathatos, in *Labrys*, 8 (1983)— a sixth letter had already appeared in *Labrys*, 5 (1979). Yet this writer thinks that a finished version of the transcribed letter may never have been mailed to Miller. Seferis was dead within the year, and there is no mention of his letter in the correspondence between Miller and Maro Seferis that is described above. The reader of the sixth letter may notice the absence of Miller's condolences to the widow of Seferis, although this apparent rudeness may reflect Miller's unconventional character persisting into old age. A similar absence of congratulations on Seferis' Nobel Prize in 1963 is more understandable. Miller was always an anti-establishment person and quite wary of official awards and recognitions.

The Seferis-Miller friendship had been unconventional from the start, when the two men met through Lawrence Durrell and George Katsimbalis in September, 1939. Seferis' *Meres C* provides us with some relevant entries which, together with the poem that Seferis dedicated to Miller, "Les anges sont blancs," help us understand the nature of that friendship. Then, there is *The Colossus of Maroussi* and the Seferis-Miller correspondence (of which only a small part has been published so far) that put matters into higher relief.

Miller was fairly well-known as an American expatriate writer living in France when he first met Seferis, on September 2, 1939, one day after the start of the Second World War (with the invasion of Poland by Germany), but Seferis had not as yet read him. He found him "clearly American, much more direct and fuller," when Miller talked of America with despair. Miller believed that, although the United States had the freest, best organized, and most varied educational system in the world, it was essentially an anti-intellectual country. On the ship bringing him to Greece from Marseille, Miller had talked to several Middle Eastern people who were enthusiastic about the progress of America, but he could not share in their enthusiasm (*Meres C*: 131-132). In *The Colossus of Maroussi* (5-7), we hear much more about that sea journey and Miller's first discovery of Greece in the person of a Greek medical student in Paris with whom he spoke in French. The subject of their conversation was paradoxically a genius of the North, the Scandinavian writer Knut Hamsun (a popular author at the time in Greece), but Miller noticed particularly that the Greeks were "an enthusiastic, curious-minded, passionate people." He had lost Passion during his years in France. Now he had found it again:

> Not only passion, but contradictoriness, confusion, chaos— all these sterling human qualities I rediscovered and cherished again in the person of my new-found friend. And generosity. I had almost thought

it had perished from the earth. There we were, a Greek and an American, with something in common, yet two vastly different beings. It was a splendid introduction to that world which was about to open before my eyes. I was almost enamored of Greece and the Greeks, before catching sight of the country. I could see in advance that they were a friendly, hospitable people, easy to reach, easy to deal with.

Miller found passion also in Seferis, but this was an introspective kind of passion that avoided overstatement. The following portrait of Seferis by Miller (Ibid.: 46-47) is a harbinger of what was written much later about Seferis by Greek and non-Greek critics. It is all the more remarkable for its intuitiveness, as Miller had at the time a very limited knowledge of Greece, Greek culture, and Seferis' work itself, which he had only known from unpolished translations.

The man who has caught this spirit of eternity which is everywhere in Greece and who has embedded it in his poems is George Seferiades, whose pen name is Seferis. I know his work only from translation, but even if I had never read his poetry I would say this is the man who is destined to transmit the flame. Seferiades is more Asiatic than any of the Greeks I met; he is from Smyrna originally but has lived abroad for many years. He is languorous, suave, vital and capable of surprising feats of strength and agility. He is the arbiter and reconciler of conflicting schools of thought and ways of life. He asks innumerable questions in a polyglot language; he is interested in all forms of cultural expression and seeks to abstract and assimilate what is genuine and fecundating in all epochs. He is passionate about his own country, his own people, not in a hidebound chauvinistic way but as a result of patient discovery following upon years of absence abroad. This passion for one's country is a special peculiarity of the intellectual Greek who has lived abroad. In other peoples I have found it distasteful, but in the Greek I find it justifiable, and not only justifiable, but thrilling, inspiring. I remember going with Seferiades one afternoon to look at a piece of land on which he thought he might build himself a bungalow. There was nothing extraordinary about the place— it was even a bit shabby and forlorn, I might say. Or rather it was, at first sight. I never had a chance to consolidate my first fleeting impression; it changed right under my eyes as he led me about like an electrified jelly-fish from spot to spot, rhapsodizing on herbs, flowers, shrubs, rocks, clay, slopes, declivities, coves, inlets and so on. Everything he looked at was Greek in a way that he had never known before leaving his country. He could look at a headland and read into it the history of the Medes, the Persians, the Dorians, the Minoans, the Atlanteans. He could also read into it some fragments of the poem which he would write in his head on the way home while plying me with questions about the New World. He was attracted by the Sibylline character of everything which met his eye. He had a way of looking forwards and backwards, of making the object of his contemplation revolve and show forth its multiple aspects. When he talked about a thing or a person or an experience he caressed it with his tongue. Sometimes he gave me the impression of being a wild boar which had broken its tusks in furious onslaughts born of love and ecstasy. In his voice there was a bruised quality as if the object of his love, his beloved Greece, had awkwardly and unwittingly mangled the shrill notes of ululation. The mellifluous Asiatic warbler had more than once been floored by an unexpected thunderbolt; his poems were becoming more and more gem-like, more compact, compressed, scintillating and revelatory. His native flexibility was responding to the cosmic laws of curvature and finitude. He had ceased going out in all directions: his lines were making the encircling movement of embrace. He had begun to ripen into the universal poet— by passionately rooting himself into the soil of his people. Wherever there is life today in Greek art, it is based on this Antaean gesture, this passion which transmits itself from heart to feet, creating strong roots which transform the body into a tree of potent beauty.

Seferis noted in *Meres C* (132) that Miller had liked his poems "Orestis" (most probably the 16th poem of his *Mythistorima*, in *Collected Poems*: 41-43) and "Mathios Paskalis" (fuller title: "Letter of Mathios Paskalis," Ibid.: 75- 77). Miller said to Seferis that he turned things inside out in his poetry. This clearly pleased Seferis, as it verified his striving for originality within the framework of the European literary tradition. In *Meres C*, Seferis limited himself to noting things about Miller with a minimum of personal comment, as when he reproduced a letter Miller had received from an admirer of his *Tropic of Cancer*— Miller had given the letter to Seferis undoubtedly as an item of curiosity (Ibid.: 138-139). Or as when Seferis described another encounter with Miller at a taverna in Athens:

> Last night, at a taverna on Agamon Square, with Miller, Antoniou, Katsimbalis. Miller certainly knows how to move about in life, even if he is ignorant of everything else. What he has earned is what he has suffered.
>
> He relates to us various stories and encounters which he had in Paris. He speaks of Balzac. He places his *Seraphita* over all his other works and believes that as a man Balzac was a failure. He claims all that, indifferent to whether he is right or wrong, and he admits it.
>
> As we were talking casually, Miller exclaimed: "Oh! I wanted so much to read that Chinese book. I looked for it two years. I even wrote to China. When the book was found, the war started and the Japanese bombed it to pieces along with the entire city. But at the end I managed to read it. Someone from England who no longer wanted it gave it to me. Just as I also gave it to someone else later. I like for valuable things to circulate."
>
> We walked back. He accompanied me home. On the way, the question of the war came up. I talked about this feeling which one sometime has, that all of these things take place as if in sleep, acted out by sleepwalkers. "Yes, it is strange," he replied, "in Paris, years ago, seeing how life becomes more and more abstract. A friend and I concluded, 'They will end up by killing themselves without realizing it. This is what is happening now.'" I wanted to ask him about something related to this, but he cut me short: "I'd prefer not to talk

so soon about this," he said and changed subjects. This impressed me.
It was as if someone had touched him on a painful spot.
(Ibid.: 141-142)

The above entry and another from three weeks later (Ibid.: 144-146) are not only significant for revealing Seferis' ambivalence about Miller but also for being seminal to the poem which Seferis dedicated to Miller:

Miller gave me to read his notes on a work he is writing about Balzac. The inclination of Henry Miller towards astrology and the apocryphal sciences is characteristic of his "Americanism"; a kind of myth in a world without a mythology, without tradition, as America is. This man who hated the Americanized way of life is a product of American society. I do not mention this as a reproach. Only, his virtues, his strength lie not where he thinks they are. One evening he told me that he had overcome the problem which destroyed Rimbaud without noticing that the world is already different [from the world of Rimbaud] and that the problem is not the same. In any case to all those I prefer this brief notation of his: "Start thus: I am not a devotee of B.— For the Human Comedy is of minor importance. I prefer that other comedy which has been labeled 'Divine' in testimony doubtless of our sublime incorrigibility..." I dare think that he begins here with a misunderstanding of the word Comedy. Yet such a beginning could have been fruitful. He is attracted by what seems great, titanic. He observes: "Work habits (of Balzac): Went to bed 8:00 p.m. after light dinner, glass or two of Vouvray avec. At work again by 2:00 a.m. Writes till 6:00 a.m. Bath for an hour. Then proof-reading and visit from publisher. From 9-12 noon writing. Breakfasts on two boiled eggs and bread. 1-6 p.m. proof again. For periods of 6 to 8 weeks would lock himself in, seeing not even closest friends. Would emerge from labors haggard and dazed, often taking trips to Corsica, Sardinia, Vienna, Russia, Italy, the French country-side etc. (of *Lettre à Madame Carraud*, Feb. 1888). When he did eat after finishing a job, it was as follows: 100 oysters, a dozen lamb-chops, a duck, a partridge, a sole etc. etc." [sic].

Something characteristic of H.M.:

"In the rough-hewn form of heavy earth, in which Balzac's soul was imprisoned, the Buddhist drama of desire was played out in a manner such as we have never witnessed in another European."

And again (cf. *Cancer*):

"The spectacle of 'Parisian civilization' which presented itself to Louis Lambert's eyes is the picture of a world in decay. The death and disintegration which Balzac sensed over a century ago has only heightened since then. Today every great city of the world stinks to high heaven and it is from this death of the world that an artist is obliged to draw inspiration." And yet he cannot stand Eliot and notes nothing about Baudelaire. These are men of another tribe for him. His favorite poet is Whitman. He mentions him further on ("Democratic Vistas").

"Time is ample, let the victors come after us. Not for nothing does evil play its part among us... Even for the treatment of the universal, in politics, metaphysics, or anything, sooner or later we come down to one single solitary soul... America has yet morally and artistically originated nothing... Someday in these states immense poets will arise and make great poems of death. The poems of life are great, but there must be the poems of the purport of life, not only in itself, but beyond itself..."

"Cet X ou je me suis autrefois heurté..." (*Louis Lambert*, p. 200).

Whatever reservations Seferis had about Miller's views, he found them interesting and worth sampling in his diary, with the probable expectation that he might eventually tap them for his own poetry. Miller's choices in reading and other graphic details also caught Seferis' attention a few days later (Ibid.: 153-154):

> Miller lent me Nijinsky's diary: p. 22, beside the sentence "I am a man of motion not of immobility," Durrell marks Miller's own sentence: "I want to stand still and dance inside."
>
> P. 86. Beside the letter of Nijinsky to Diaghilev, Miller notes: "Copy out in hand on fine vellum. Copy this and frame it. The man who wrote this letter was no madman! He was nearer to being a god!"
>
> P. 114: "I am the one who dies when he is not loved." Miller has written: "H.; endorsed." Miller notes: "Only a few books I can read over and over again— inexhaustible joy and wisdom." These are: Lao Tse; [...?]; *Voice of Silence*; *Leaves of Grass*; Mysteries; Nijinsky; Elie Faure; Rimbaud. *Not*: Dante; Homer; Virgil; Goethe; Racine; Corneille; etc.

When Seferis and Miller exchanged opinions on writers and books, they seemed to agree on points concerning Nijinsky, but they disagreed on those concerning Dostoevsky. This made Seferis realize that Miller's religion was acceptance "to follow the direction of one's fate."

Miller certainly made an impression on Seferis. On January 4, 1940, Seferis remembers in his diary his last meeting with Miller on Christmas Eve and records his last words before he sailed off to America. When he comes back to Miller in his diary, shortly after, he tries to sum up his impressions of the strange American:

> Henry Miller said: "I am not a writer" and claimed, not from a sense of pessimism, but rather optimism, that all art was going to die in time (Durrell interpreted this to mean "our kind of art."). That is a characteristic utterance of a man for whom eternity does not exist, or rather, *his* eternity is not in his work, but elsewhere. He also said: "I am not a writer, I am a man." He hated anything mechanical, abstract.

He was a man crazy with excitement at having found his voice. When you know what this means, you understand what may happen to someone who feels that God gave him a voice of his own; that he created him, too, a man with voice. H.M. gives you sometimes the impression that he is like a plant. I would like to accord this word the best possible meaning. It is an admirable feature of his; no longer *man* (in general) but *a man*, under a [general] human surface, sticking out, when he can return from the bottom, a strangely moulded and still muddy head. (Ibid.: 162)

There is only one other man whose pronouncements, profound or trivial, Seferis has recorded with almost piety— Eliot, a man very different from Miller. Eliot's example and work had of course a much greater influence on Seferis than had Miller's, but we must note that while the Eliot-Seferis relationship developed as a rather formal teacher-disciple connection, and Seferis' correspondence with Eliot was scanty and conventional— Seferis' exchanges with Miller and their correspondence were quite warm, far-ranging, and open-minded. On the whole, the two men functioned as intellectual partners. As a French critic, here translated, has rightly noted, "The qualities that Miller found among the Greeks, courage, frankness, spiritual strength, humanity... compensating for the poverty of European civilization, were the very ones in which Seferis believed... For Seferis, the integrity... of Miller made him important to contemporary Greece" (Kohler 1985: 585).

It is strange that nowhere in *Meres C* does Seferis refer to Miller's gift of the manuscript about Greece that was later printed as *First Impressions of Greece*. He certainly read it (although we do not know exactly when), as the manuscript bears pencil marks on the margin, beside particular passages or turns of phrase that obviously drew his attention. But why did he not discuss it in his diary? Probably because it mirrored what he already knew of Miller's personality and mind from their meetings, and then, as Seferis has observed, a diary is an incomplete and fragmentary record of things (*Meres C*: 178).

Another peculiarity is that Seferis never disclosed to Miller that he had written and inscribed a poem, "Les anges sont blancs," to him. Miller learned about it many years later through Kimon Friar (see below). The poem figures in the collection *Logbook I* (*Collected Poems*: 255-259), placed third from the end, before "The Decision to Forget" and "The King of Asine," and must have been written shortly before or after Miller's departure from Greece. It was first printed about that time in the journal *Nea Grammata*. We can only speculate on the reasons why Seferis kept his poem secret from Miller.

III

"Les anges sont blancs"
To Henry Miller

Tout à coup Louis cessa de frotter ses jambes l'une contre l'autre et dit d'une voix lente: "Les anges sont blancs."

> Like a sailor in the shrouds he slipped over the tropic of
>   Cancer and the tropic of Capricorn
> and it was natural he couldn't stand before us at a man's
>   height
> but looked at us all from the height of a fire-fly or from the
>   height of a pine tree
> drawing his breath deeply in the dew of the stars or in the
>   dust of the earth.
> Naked women with bronze leaves from a Barbary fig tree
>   surrounded him
> extinguished lamp posts airing stained bandages of the
>   great city
> ungainly bodies producing Centaurs and Amazons
>   when their hair touched the Milky Way.
> And days have passed since the first moment he greeted us
>   taking his head off and placing it on the iron table
> while the shape of Poland changed like ink drunk by
>   blotting-paper
> and we journeyed among shores of islands bare like strange

fish bones on the sand
and the whole sky, empty and white, was a pigeon's huge
    wing beating with a rhythm of silence
and dolphins under the colored water turned dark quickly
    like the soul's movements
like movements of the imagination and the hands of men
    who grope and kill themselves in sleep
in the huge unbroken rind of sleep that wraps around us
    common to all of us, our common grave
with brilliant minute crystals crushed by the motion of
    reptiles.
And yet everything was white because the great sleep is
    white and the great death
calm and serene and isolated in an endless silence.
And the cackling of the guinea-hen at dawn and the cock
    that crowed falling into a deep well
and the fire on the mountain-side raising hands of sulphur
    and autumn leaves
and the ship with its forked shoulder-blades more tender
    than our first lovemaking,
all were things isolated even beyond the poem
that you abandoned when you fell heavily along with its
    last word
knowing nothing any longer among the white eyeballs
    of the blind and the sheets
that you unfolded in fever to cover the daily procession
of people who fail to bleed even when they strike themselves
    with axes and nails;
they were things isolated, put somewhere else, and the steps
    of whitewash
descended to the threshold of the past and found silence and
    the door didn't open
and it was as if your friends, in great despair, knocked
    loudly and you were with them

but you heard nothing and dolphins rose around you
>   dumbly in the seaweed.
And again you gazed intently and that man, the teethmarks
>   of the tropics in his skin,
putting on his dark glases as if he were going to work with
>   a blowlamp,
said humbly, pausing at every word:
"The angels are white flaming white and the eye that would
>   confront them shrivels
and there's no other way you've got to become like stone if
>   you want their company
and when you look for the miracle you've got to scatter your
>   blood to the eight points of the wind
because the miracle is nowhere but circulating in the veins
>   of man."

Hydra—Athens, November, 1939

The reference to the island of Hydra helps us understand some of the poem's imagery; the dedication to Miller helps unlock other allusions, and the epigraph from Balzac accounts for the strange title and helps us with the conclusion of the poem. Even so, without *Meres C* and some deep pondering, "Les anges sont blancs" would still remain a mysterious poem, hard to decipher or make sense of. This probably explains why the critics of Seferis have not discussed it. The only analysis that exists, by C. Capri-Karka in *War in the Poetry of George Seferis* (91-101), is helpful but uneven. Capri-Karka rightly parallels Balzac's *Louis Lambert* and Miller of *Tropic of Cancer* in reference to the confusion and downgrading of values in our modern world. She points out the allusions in the poem to Miller, the man obsessed with sex and restlessness, and throws light upon the sleep-walking, the senseless killing motif, by reference to *Meres C* (see relevant entry above) and Seferis' essay on Artemidorus on the interpretation of dreams (in *Dokimes*, II: 311-332), where, in fact, Seferis quotes "Les anges sont blancs" as an illustration of his discussion of dreams.

But the analysis becomes idle when the lines "he greeted us/ taking his head off and placing it on the iron table" are termed surrealistic[1] and explained as an allusion to "man's disintegration." For Seferis the image must have been much more sensual and real, not a totally mental conception. The "iron table" is the round iron table (in the shape of an ancient tripod), a trademark of pre-war cafés in Greece.[2] Seferis, Katsimbalis, and Miller must have sat around such tables more than once and held far-ranging conversations with the help of ouzo or Greek wine. The man who "takes off his head and places it on the iron table" is Miller, the open, uninhibited, and unpretentious man who disclosed his innermost self to his Greek friends— Miller's main point of attraction to Seferis.

Another point that Capri-Karka seems to have missed in her survey of the poem is that Miller, whom she calls the "protagonist" of the poem, is no longer the same man who hides behind the "you" of the second part. This is the poet who talks to himself, whose nightmarish state of mind is in fact the focus of "Les anges sont blancs." Miller reappears at the end, as the man with "the teethmarks/ of the tropics in his skin," to pronounce his Sibylline oracle. This conclusion is where the narrator-poet (Seferis) and the prophet-madman (Miller-Lambert) coincide and become fused. The words in quotation marks are not an exact reproduction of what Miller had said to Seferis, but rather the sum of his personality and ideology codified in imagery that centers around Louis Lambert's "white angels." The phrase "white angels" is the most difficult point in the poem, a paradoxical utterance of a madman or of a seemingly mad hero of Balzac, which the modern poet borrows to make the cornerstone of his poem and is obliged to interpret in his own way.

It was the habit of Seferis, when he borrowed something from previous literature, to metamorphose and reinterpret it in the light of his own text. Capri-Karka attempts to explain the "white angels," partly, by reference to Seferis' other uses of the notion "angel" in his poetry. The survey proves that each use of "angel" bears a different coloration, but does not explain "les anges blancs" of the poem. The intensity here of Seferis' "white" is found in the poem itself: "the angels are white flaming white." It is not the "white" opposite of "black," but the intense "white" sometimes called "red hot," the truer face of reality that, to recall Eliot, humans could not bear to look at, the look of the ancient Gorgon that petrified anyone who dared to face her.

Like many other poems of Seferis, "Les anges sont blancs" displays free association of disparate elements, but is a work uniform in mood and spirit, that fits in well with the other poems framing it at the end of *Logbook I*. Balzac's *Louis Lambert* interpreted by Henry Miller suggested to Seferis both the title and the central idea of the poem. Critics of Balzac have spoken of his "angelism," the tendency to idealize disincarnation (not incarnation), or flesh-become-word. In *Louis Lambert*, which is the philosophical essence of *La Comédie Humaine*, the hero, Lambert, is so poor at communicating that he appears crazy to others. Lambert (in Seferis' mind) turns into Miller, a mouthpiece of the unknown. He is seized or inspired by a god or a demon. Like the Delphic Pythia or the Cumaean Sibyl, Miller is half-conscious of the meaning of his words. He transmits an oracle to Seferis who ponders and analyzes it. Seferis does so, while holding true to Miller's dictum about him— that he turns things inside out. "White" is divested of its positive associations, and is twisted around to mean something accursed (just as the Greek term *semnos* can mean both "sacred" and "accursed"). The same method (as the present writer has shown) was applied by Seferis elsewhere, e.g. to demythologize the Romantic symbol of the swans, or to indicate by "honey of the sun" the notion of entrapment rather than of enjoyment.[3]

"White" as predicative of "Angels" is the emphatic word of the poem's title, and inside the poem it is used in a contrastive manner, to mean both "blazing" or "unbearably hot," and "empty" or "deadly vacuous." Such explicit or implicit contrasts abound in the poetry of Seferis, as, for instance, in the "light, angelic and black" of *Thrush* (*Collected Poems*: 337). Here, the idea of monstrous antithesis is introduced first by the portrait of Miller, who confronts his Greek friends not "at a man's height" but "from the height of a fire-fly or from the/ height of a pine tree/ drawing his breath deeply in the dew of the stars or in the/ dust of the earth," and is surrounded by animalistic figures (Centaurs and Amazons) whose hair, however, touches the Milky Way. Then "white" acts as an axis of contrast: "the whole sky, empty and white"; "everything was white because the great sleep is/ white"; "the white eyeballs/ of the blind." Even the serene, whitewashed staircases of Hydra function in the poet's mind as staircases to the closed door of memory.[4] Reality is round like the earth and like the universe. Overexcess of life leads to no life. The point is how to balance these opposites. Seferis had already put the question in the poem "Man" of his series *Stratis the Mariner Describes a Man*: "What can a flame remember? If it remembers a little less than is necessary, it goes out; if it remembers a little more than is necessary, it goes out. If only it could teach us, while it burns, to remember correctly." (*Collected Poems*: 147).

In the conclusion of "Les anges sont blancs," Miller endorses for Seferis a Dionysiac kind of abandon, where death is accepted as part of the game of life, of the miracle of regeneration: "there's no other way you've got to become like stone if/ you want their company/ and when you look for the miracle you've got to scatter your/ blood to the eight points of the wind/ because the miracle is nowhere but circulating in the veins/ of man." Many years later, another author, Nikos Gabriel Pentzikis, challenged Seferis more directly. He declared that Seferis could not or did not want to "get up and dance off" his existential anxieties. "Seferis' poetry," he added, "does not end with otherwordly interests. He does not overcome anxiety by accepting ugliness." (*Ya ton Seferi* 1961: 154). It does not matter that Pentzikis and Miller were poles apart otherwise. What is significant is that both authors tested Seferis' view of life. What is more significant is that Seferis was sufficiently broadminded and sensitive to notice and respond to the messages of the two authors who challenged him. The message of Miller was recorded without apparent acceptance or rejection in this poem, "Les anges sont blancs."

This brings us back to the question of why Seferis withheld from Miller the existence of the poem. Our analysis suggests the answer. The poem was not a celebration of Miller, as the Rex Warner poem was a celebration of Warner (*Collected Poems*: 433-437). It was inscribed to Miller because it derives from conversations Seferis had with Miller and because the personality of the American looms large in it. Miller was a generous spirit, as Seferis knew him to be, but no one is completely unbiased or capable of accepting all opinions about oneself. One reason why Miller gave short shrift to the English in his *The Colossus of Maroussi* was certainly the negative criticism his works had provoked in Britain. The portrait of Miller in "Les anges sont blancs" matches his portrait in Seferis' *Meres C*. Seferis saw Miller, his senior by several years, as a brilliant child-man, half-conscious of the truths he utters, "sticking out, when he can return from the bottom, a strangely moulded and still muddy head." Seferis did not dismiss Miller as an odd American expatriate with half-baked ideas; he was impressed by him. There nevertheless was a touch of condescension in the way he saw Miller. In "Les anges sont blancs," the words and gestures of Miller were used in a dispassionate, almost clinical fashion, to illustrate Seferis' Kafkaesque state of mind during the first part of the Second World War— the poem alluded to Poland being invaded by Germany: "while the shape of Poland changed like ink drunk by/ blotting paper." Seferis must have wondered how Miller would have taken all this and whether the poem would cost him Miller's friendship. Perhaps this is why he did not mention the poem in his correspondence with Miller.

IV

Miller knew that Seferis was very interested in America and curious about the American mentality and social conditions, the place of blacks in American society, and American writers and artists in particular. The subject of America came up immediately after the two men met and started corresponding, e.g. in a letter from Miller to Seferis, dated September 15, 1939 at Corfu. In this letter, which was typewritten probably on Durrell's typewriter and bears corrections in handwriting, Miller wrote about American writers and proclaimed that the only truly great American poet was Whitman. The point on Whitman was reflected, as we have seen, in Seferis' *Meres C*.

Soon after his return to America, in early 1940, Miller started travelling around his homeland out of curiosity, undoubtedly reinforced by his many years of self-exile in Europe. He sent a card to Seferis from Richmond, Virginia, where he had stopped to see Poe's home, "one of them," as he put it. Then he sent a long handwritten letter, dated February 22, 1940, from New York. This letter seems to continue the process started in Greece, Miller's trying to educate Seferis in American culture:

My dear Seferiades:

Just a brief word to confirm the poetic impressions of n.y. which you got thru [sic] the writings. I have just come in. Midnight. Living in same hotel with Sherwood Anderson (whom I have met and found somewhat disappointing— he and Dos Passos both together). Anyway, what made me think of you was seeing Louis Armstrong's Club advertised *on Broadway* now (the Cotton Club) as being "TERRIFIC." I wanted to go in and report on it for you, but didn't have the price. But I will soon— and it looks promising from the billboards outside. There is a "terrific" almost pre-war atmosphere here— different generation, of course. But jammed with bars, lounges, shows, dives, dance halls— our very little block contains more night life than all Athens— and there are thousands of blocks, so it seems. An atmosphere of spending, of a gayety that I don't care for, but gay, reckless, heedless— Alexandrian, in a sense— an American sense, of course. Deep lanes of most brilliant neon lights in all colors— one great big Wrigley Chewing Gum electric display that I swear is a combination (in electric colors) of Reichel and Paul Klee— fishes swimming in electric sperm— really better than the American art galleries! (Takes in a whole block.)

 I walked the streets for an hour or so tonight, exactly as I walked in "Capricorn"— past all the old places (still going strong) and felt even more alone than before— but not *lonely* now. But "broken" as usual. If they only knew what I had written, I keep thinking. I am walking along without a cent again— only a temporary affair and nothing to worry about— but still, nobody has painted the scene as I have, I own it, so to speak, and I am on the outside looking in, like a tramp. Only now it doesn't disturb me in the least. Now I am living in a hotel, like a traveller— that *is* progress, for me. I like that very much. I am not at home here. Nobody knows my address. I have a room I like, with space enuf [sic] to do my yoga exercises. The heat is bountiful— the bathroom luxurious. I may actually begin to write. The fact that I am writing you and Durrell and Katsimbalis is a good sign. Anyway, I was thinking of you warmly this evening. At least *you* would have enjoyed it, had you been with me. You would probably go crazy. The scale is so tremendous no words will do. One has to do what Picasso did in his "Guernica."

Not the least interesting is the display of books, piled up like confetti in little shops sandwiched in amidst burlesque houses, hosiery shops, bars, etc. Books in cloth cover, good print, fine paper, endless subject matter, from 35 cents up. Incredible. Same goes for leather goods. I've seen a million bags I'd like to buy. And then troupes of unescorted girls of all ages, out having a good time with their own money. Strange sight— like pictures of the African veldt demonstrating Kropotkin's theory of "mutual aid" among the different animal species. At midnight tonight, from 42nd to 57th streets, along B'way or Seventh Avenue, *no less* than a million people parading. All laughing. The war is there in the newspapers. We are billions of miles away. I look at the faces— maybe I am wrong, but they seem not only callous, but unreachable. One good bombing of n.y. and all would change. I would almost like to see it. It would be "TERRIFIC"— "COLOSSAL."

Always yours,
Miller

P.S. I asked Laughlin to send you the Rimbaud translation several weeks ago. Hope you receive it. Will be sending other things too.

The letter has a youthful sloppiness about it. In the manuscript[5] even the pages are wrongly numbered and the postscript is scribbled sideways, on one of the middle pages. Laughlin was Miller's New Directions publisher, James Laughlin.

The debonaire attitude of Miller towards the war, which at that time was raging in Europe, can be understood on the basis of his past experiences.

Miller had already gone through many wars, both in the outside world and in his mind. He had developed what a Greek would call *anosia* ("immunity to disease"; here, "indifference to pain"). The same attitude motivated him later to urge Seferis (when the latter was in South Africa, due to the war) to drop everything and go explore Timbuctoo!

The subject of the war came up again in a Miller letter dated May 31, 1940. Miller foretold that his country would eventually enter the war and win it. In the same letter, Seferis was sent a few pages of what Miller called his "essay on Greece" (that is, *The Colossus of Maroussi*). With his letter of June 25, 1940, Miller sent to Seferis the entire first part of his "essay" with the request that he pass it on to Katsimbalis after reading it. On August 21, 1940, he sent another chapter, and on October 15, 1940, he sent the last two parts and informed Seferis that he had not yet secured a publisher, although several were interested. The first two letters of Seferis to Miller were in French. Seferis' response to Miller's letter of August 21, 1940, is the first surviving English letter. It was dated October 8, 1940. It was one of the six letters published by J. Stathatos in *Labrys*, 8, as mentioned above. In that letter Seferis said that he took Miller's typescript of *The Colossus* to the hill (Areopagus) opposite the Acropolis to read it under a "very rigorous sun." He went on to say:

> As I turned over your pages I felt the same sensation growing in me, which I had when hearing for the first time Louis Armstrong one foggy night in London. There upon the rock, between some short pine trees and cactuses the negro face with pearls of sweat rolling upon its cheeks, was dancing round me like the head of a modern saint. My cares and sorrows, which are sometimes now rather heavy, went away— gone really gone— my dear friend, with the sound of the enormous trumpet shining in the sky like the sun. Thanks to you, I had at least one marvelous morning hour. And that in these wretched days we are living, is a very important thing to me.
> (Ibid.: 52)

The reference to jazz had to do with the fact that Miller had jokingly named the part of *The Colossus* in question "Boogie Woogie Passacaglia" and with Seferis' own love of jazz.

In the meantime Greece, invaded by Mussolini, had repulsed the enemy against all odds. These events seem to have elated even the usually gloomy Seferis. A draft of a telegram by him to Miller, dated November 7, 1940, ten days after the Italian invasion, suggests both Seferis' indignation at the unjustified assault (preceded by other covert acts of war) and his enthusiasm at the heroic resistance of the Greek army:

> Fighting against brutal invader for
> our souls for everything you loved
> here. Support your friends. Hearty
> salute.   — George Seferiades.

Even if we can assume that Seferis did send Miller the above message, Miller may never have received it, as he had already departed from New York without leaving a forwarding address. He had borrowed money and started his wanderings around America in an effort to come to terms with his own people. Seferis' life was turned upside down. When the Germans invaded Greece in the spring of 1941, he and his wife followed the Greek government in its retreat to first Crete and then Egypt. Still later, Seferis was posted for a few months to the Greek embassy in South Africa. It was from Johannesburg that Seferis seems to have written to Miller on August 2, 1941, judging from Miller's letter to Seferis, dated October 3, 1941, from Chicago. The letter, on stationery from the Hotel Mayer of Elko, Nevada, is as exuberant as the letter from New York printed above:

> My dear Seferiades,
>
> Your letter from Johannesburg dated the second of August [1941] just reached me here on my way back to New York. Two months' time, as you see, but not so bad, considering the times. I write you immediately in the hope this will reach you somewhere. Have heard nothing of course from Katsimbalis or anyone in Greece. Had a letter from Larry [Durrell] (Cairo) dated May, I believe, saying that Katsimbalis was a prisoner of war and that [Theodore] Stephanides had been killed—but no word of Antoniou. I do hope he has been spared. That's the last news from anyone, and where Larry is now I don't know.
> *The Colossus* is due to appear this week and I am instructing the publisher to send you several copies (you may want some for your friends) to Johannesburg. Hope they get there! I will have the Hamlet (Vol. 2) sent to you also, and the "Wisdom of the

Heart" when it comes out in November. I had a small essay published privately in book form, called "The World of Sex," but doubt if it would get through the censor. If you think so, I will send you a copy. In all, four books so far this year— possibly a fifth. A good year for publishing, but dull otherwise. I have been on my tour just a year now and the book on America is nearly done. I can't say that the trip was very exciting. More like a year wasted— except that it satisfied an old craving and corroborated my intuitions.

I had a good stay in Hollywood— about four months. Met a number of famous movie stars, including John Barrymore and Luise Rainer, and lots of writers of course. I must say that I liked California more than any other State, largely because of the climate and scenery. It is cheap to live there too. If you ever get to America you must go there. You will make friends quickly— it is more like Europe than any place in America. No doubt you have Greek friends there, or certainly friends from Paris. I met a number of people there whom I knew in Paris, including Man Ray, the photographer, and Max Ernst, the painter. It's an easy Paradisiac life there— almost too easy. Had I wanted I could have taken a job in the movies— was offered jobs by three different companies, but refused to be tempted. They pay colossal wages— from one hundred dollars to 2,000 dollars per week! But the work is terrible and the life is ghastly. You pay for it in the end.

What impresses me most about the trip, looking back on it now, is the West. Once you cross the Mississippi River you are in a new world, and at times a terrifying world. Past the Rocky Mountains it is still different. And enormous like travelling over the surface of a dead planet. States like Arizona, New Mexico, Montana, Idaho, Texas, etc., are unimaginable until you see them. Room enough for all the world, it seems. California has everything— everything that man needs. In fact, a superabundance of everything.

Naturally, people with all the comforts are not crazy about

going to war. My impression, in travelling about the country, is that the Americans do not want to go to war at all. They are indifferent to the fate of Europe. It is too remote for them. How it will all end I do not know. Now it seems as if Russia were holding her own— but for how long?

You were lucky in a way to have escaped to another country. I have met some interesting poets there. No doubt you have met them already. Anyway, the primitive peoples ought to be interesting. Do let me know where you go next, so that I may keep in touch with you. My address (below) is a permanent mail address, no matter where I go. I think to stay in N.Y. a month or two and then go to Mexico. But I will keep in touch with you. I am delighted to have heard from you. I have a feeling you will eventually be coming this way, perhaps via South America. I will also see that you get some books, beside my own. And if you succeed in getting in touch with Katsimbalis and Ghika and the others, do give them my warm regards. More when I get to New York!

Always yours,
Henry Miller

[P.S.] Address me care of [...]. How is your sister Jeanne? I enclose an announcement of "Colossus" from the publisher— will be a fine printing job!

In her book *My Brother George Seferis*, Ioanna Tsatsos (whom Miller called "Jeanne," *à la française*) provides a very positive portrait of Miller, stressing his spontaneity and unpretentious humanity. And in Bertrand Mathieu, "Henry Miller. The 40 Years of the 'Colossus'" *Tomes*, 59 (April, 1980), 4-12 [in Greek], Mrs. Tsatsos says that she was struck in 1939 at how youthful Miller seemed; his outlook was fresh and he was disposed to giving all of himself; a "gangster-author," as he described himself on the back of a photograph. Miller also drew a very flattering portrait of Ioanna Tsatsos and other Greek women in *The Colossus of Maroussi*.

The 1941 publication notice of *The Colossus* from Colt Press, San Francisco, calls this work "the finest and most joyous book ever written about the people and the land of Greece" and "a stirring contemporary account of the great spirit of a nation, which, at the very time of writing, was heroically resisting the forces of Fascism. Here one of America's most distinguished writers distills into warm discursive prose the living magnificence of this ancient land!" This reads like an unconscious response to the telegram of Seferis to Miller, and the comments on Greece may have been suggested by Miller himself.

Seferis replied to the above letter on November 27, 1941, and then (unsure of whether Miller had received his letter) on December 25, 1941, both times from South Africa. In the latter letter (which has been published in *Meres D*: 169-171, and in *Labrys*, 5 (1979)), Seferis says that he has not received as yet *The Colossus*, but finds the opportunity to enlighten Miller on the events of the previous year and the fate of their common friends: the poet Antoniou, Nancy and Lawrence Durrell, Bernard Spencer, and Katsimbalis. It was not true that Stephanides had been killed or that Katsimbalis was a prisoner of war. He also supplied news of his sister Ioanna, who had stayed in Greece with her family. Miller seems to have received Seferis' letter very quickly. He wrote back from New York City on January 29, 1942, hoping that Seferis had gotten the three copies of *The Colossus* that he had sent him. He also gave a thought to Greece: "Yes, it must be frightful in Greece now. I know we [the Americans] are trying to send shiploads of food." Miller predicts that the allies will win the war, but then, he says, there will be a revolution. America will emerge as the most reactionary country in the world, "as indeed we are," he adds. Other comments in this letter also have to be taken with a grain of salt: life in Cairo for Durrell and all the others ought to be exciting, and Seferis should take advantage of his time on the Black Continent. "I wish you could explore Africa a bit. A great continent. I would a thousand times rather be there than here. Go to *Timbuctoo*. Don't worry..."

"You say to Seferis: 'Go to Timbuctoo.' But Seferis says: 'No joy, no inspiration. We are in the game and eaten by the game,'" Seferis wrote on March 7, 1942 (in *Labrys*, 8: 53-54). Seferis was still in South Africa but expecting to move back to Cairo. The letter was started on the 7th, resumed on the 8th, and finished on the 11th of March. Seferis had received L.C. Powell's book, *Robinson Jeffers: The Man and his Work*, from Miller and was reading it: "This book with your own notes moved me. I [remember] your ways of giving: a plain and whole gesture— and my reading in Athens of Nijinsky's diary with your scribbling upon the margins." The next paragraph of this letter is reserved for *The Colossus*, one copy of which Seferis had gotten from Colt Press. His comment on the book is brief but telling: "It has been like [a] rainbow against the sky."

V

Seferis was not to write another letter to Miller until 1948. As he wrote in *Thrush*: "The times/ happened to be unpropitious: war, destruction, exile." (*Collected Poems*: 319). Miller proved more forthcoming. A 1943 Christmas card came to Seferis from Miller, and then a May 28, 1945 letter (Seferis was back in Greece by that time), with a salut! "Mille fois salut! Et pax vobiscum! What an age since we have heard from one another!" Miller was also curious as to whether Katsimbalis had yet read *The Colossus of Maroussi*. Communications had been difficult. Seferis took time before writing back to Miller, although on October 21, 1944 (while sailing back to Greece from Italy) he thought of doing so: "Last night I finished reading *Lost Traveller*. I feel (first time in years) like writing to Miller who has not forgotten me. I hope he may sympathize with me for not answering his messages" (*Meres D*: 369).

In 1947 Seferis obtained through Lawrence Durrell a recording of Miller reading from his works. He invited some of his friends to listen to Miller's voice. Then, in 1948, *The King of Asine and Other Poems* appeared in England and Miller was sent a copy. This event and an unexpected visit Miller received from Seferis' younger brother Angelos, who was teaching English at Monterey, California, prompted Miller to resume his correspondence with Seferis. He wrote from Big Sur, California, on October 3, 1948, saying that he had not heard from Seferis for many years and did not know whether he was dead or alive. He did not even know that Seferis had married in 1940, shortly before his evacuation to Crete.

Seferis' reply to this letter, dated December 7, 1948, and mailed from

Ankara, Turkey, where he was then serving in the Greek Embassy, has been printed in *Labrys*, 8 (1983), and, before that, in *The Coffeehouse*, 9 (1979). It is one of the most moving of all the letters that Seferis wrote to Miller. He picks up the thread of their relationship from Miller's suggestion, in 1942, that he go and explore Timbuctoo. "Cairo and the whole Middle-East affair has been a long nightmare to me," he says. "As I recall the past, I think that the happiest day of my life during the recent years was the day when, on board of a military transport, I felt that we were on the doorstep of Greece [in October, 1944], you know, the moment when the voyage ceases to be horizontal and becomes a sort [of] virginal ascension." Back in Greece, Seferis had to endure the horrors of the second round of the Greek civil war. "If you can imagine the ugliest thing against the most perfect sky of our planet, you'll understand if I tell you that I have experienced the sharpest tragedy a human being could experience. The light itself was bleeding." But there were, later on, some pleasant moments, as when Larry (Lawrence Durrell) brought the recording of Miller's voice reading some pages from *Tropic of Capricorn*. Seferis confirmed that he had married and reminded Miller of the fact that he (that is, Miller) had met the woman in Seferis' apartment in Athens. There was a touch of good-natured irony when Seferis imagined Miller getting on with his "titanic work." Miller had written that he was finishing at the time *The Rosy Crucifixion*.

In his follow-up letter, dated March 9, 1949, Miller informed Seferis, among other things, that *The Colossus* had caught the interest of the French: "Everyone in France loves the *Colosse de Maroussi*." Miller wondered whether this work would ever come out in Greece? Seferis had translated a few pages of it, but the entire work finally appeared in Greece in a translation by A. Karandonis, the critic who had first noticed and promoted the poetry of Seferis in Greece. Miller finished his letter with an affectionate "Je t'embrasse."

Angelos Seferiades, Seferis' brother, died suddenly on January 19, 1950, and this was the immediate occasion for Miller's next letter to Seferis. "A shock to hear of his death after the burial," he wrote on January 22, 1950, also acknowledging receipt of Seferis' New Year greetings. In another letter that he sent four months later (dated May 7, 1950), Miller said he had read three thick volumes by Schliemann (the excavator of Troy and Mycenae) and wondered whether Seferis had gone to see the seven buried cities of Troy? Seferis had been stationed in Turkey since the end of 1948. Miller was also curious to know whether Schliemann's museum in Berlin had been ruined by the bombings of the city. The "palace" that Schliemann had built for himself and his dear [wife] Sophie in Athens, where was it located?[6]

An April 24, 1954, letter of Miller to Seferis seems to have been prompted by Miller's receiving a copy in translation of "Les anges sont blancs" from Kimon Friar, who was then translating a number of Greek poems by various hands. "First I knew of it [i.e., the poem], or where to reach you (Durrell wrote too saying that you had paid him a visit in Cyprus.)," Miller said, and went on to inform Seferis about the French translations of his own works. Seferis' reply to this letter was sent two weeks later (dated May 8, 1954) and has been printed in *Labrys*, 8 (1983). Seferis had been serving as Ambassador at the Greek Legation in Beirut, Lebanon, since the end of 1952, after the one and a half years of service in England that followed his service in Turkey. He made a short stopover on Cyprus while on his way to Beirut, and then visited the island again for a month in 1953, when he met Durrell, who was teaching English in Nicosia. Durrell had bought a house in the Kerynia district and was thinking of settling on Cyprus for an indefinite time. Seferis also informed Miller that *The Colossus*, "more Katsimbalistic than ever, has taken the plane for the States; is now in the States; is already ruminating American stories. I am trying to imagine your meeting in Big Sur and I can't help considering it one of the greatest events of the century." As for the poem to Miller, Seferis said that it was "an old one... made out of impressions from" their "journey to Hydra and inspired from a reading" of Miller's "notes on Balzac." He did not know what sort of feeling Friar's translation might convey. He himself did not believe in translations, although he would be happy to receive any of the French translations of Miller's books.

When Seferis was dating the above letter, however, Miller had already seen Katsimbalis, who seems to have travelled rapidly despite his large size. This is evident from the following brief letter, dated May 7, 1954, which Miller sent to Seferis:

My dear George,

Katsimbalis was here— for just 2 days, alas!— and seemed more "colossal" than ever. I sat and listened to him for the whole 48 hours. We talked of you, naturally, and he told me of your book, *Three Days in Cappadocia*. I want very much to read it. Can you send me a copy or tell me where I may buy it, whether in French, German or English.[7] Just read Rex Warner's translation of Xenophon— same general territory. Fascinated by it. We shan't leave here until September at least, if we do go abroad. And we *may* go first to Japan and India. Will let you know more later. This is in haste, but with affection.

Henry Miller

Seferis had already posted the French edition of his travelogue on Cappadocia to Miller, and Miller thanked him for the book with a card dated October 7, 1954. The card was made from a photo of Miller and his friend, the painter Emil White, embracing. The caption says: "Midnight 1952." The photo-card was sent, it seems, in exchange for a photo of Seferis and Durrell in Cyprus that Seferis had sent to Miller with his May 8, 1954, letter.

Three years later, when Seferis was appointed Greek Ambassador to Britain, Miller wrote him lightheartedly, on May 2, 1957:

I never thought I could live to see the day when I could say "my friend so-and-so is now an Ambassador!" Hurrah! Hurrah! But watch your step, George! Don't let the English trip you or lead you into a trap.

Miller's "war" with England was an old story, as shown in the discussion above about "Les anges sont blancs." In *The Colossus of Maroussi* Miller drew a damning portrait of the English, and as late as 1978, he called England "bloody" in discussing his friend Durrell (*Labrys*, 5 (1979), 79).

Three Miller letters to Seferis, dating from 1958 (April 3, April 24, and June 12), had to do with an act of charity by Miller. In *The Colossus*, Miller described meeting and befriending a Cretan called Alexandros at Phaistos, a site on Crete that enraptured him. It seems that the custodian of the site, named

Alexandros, mistook Miller for a typical monied American, and when they later corresponded, he asked for financial help. It was not unusual for Greeks in the late 1940s, ravaged as they were from several years of war (against Germany and then civil war), to look towards America as a potential source of material assistance. Miller shipped Alexandros several packages of clothing, and in the last of the three letters mentioned above, he said that he wanted to help Alexandros to buy some land. He hoped that Seferis might assist him in this exchange. The next item in the Seferis-Miller correspondence seems to be a card from Miller, dated July 21, 1963, in which he congratulated Seferis on his retirement from the diplomatic service. Miller was glad that his friend was again "a free man" and advised him to write more poems.

Many years passed before there was any contact between the two men, who were destined never to see each other again after Seferis said goodbye to Miller in 1939. Seferis was awarded the Nobel Prize for Literature in 1963, but Miller's reaction is unknown. Seferis also traveled to the United States twice in the 1960s, to accept an honorary doctorate at Princeton University, in 1965, and then in 1968, to spend time at the Princeton Institute for Advanced Study and give readings of his poetry at Princeton and other universities, as well as at the Poetry Centre in New York City. Miller remained in California and Seferis did not travel to the West Coast. It was again Miller, the more aggressive of the two, who took the initiative and re-established contact after reading Seferis' interview with Keeley in *The Paris Review*, as mentioned at the beginning of this chapter.

In 1978 Miller was still living. Mrs. Maro Seferis wrote him (on October 10) enquiring about Seferis' letters to him. Could Miller supply copies of these letters to John Stathatos, who was preparing an edition of the entire Seferis-Miller correspondence? Seferis had kept carbon copies of his letters to others, but some of these copies had faded considerably and others might be missing. If Miller provided new copies, the publication of the Seferis-Miller correspondence would be complete. Miller had already donated his papers to the U.C.L.A. Library, and in a brief answer to Mrs. Seferis, dated November 22, 1978, promised to search for any of Seferis' letters and send her whatever he could find; and, either from senility or because he was trying to be humorous, he added: "But if George kept all his letters I don't expect to find any." At the time, Miller had outlived Seferis for as many years as Seferis was his junior.

VI

Self-pity and a sense of tragedy pervade Seferis' verse, but these are more directly expressed in some of the epigraphs which he chose for his collections of poems (see, for instance, *Collected Poems*: 203, 317, 451, 479). There is always an underlying question, whether poetry is worth writing, whether communication among human beings is at all possible. Yet Seferis went on writing, throwing bottles into the sea, as he put it; shoring fragments of life against his ruins, as Eliot would have put it. In Balzac's *Louis Lambert*, pointed out to him by Miller, Seferis may have recognized himself minus his self-control, or, at least, his ability to sublimate his sorrows in his literary work.

We could not, in fact, imagine Seferis without his writing: his poetry, essays, and diaries. These were useful to him as lifelines to sanity. Miller was himself a writer, in fact a more compulsive writer than Seferis, especially when viewed by an outsider. Yet oddly enough, writing seemed incidental to this 50-year-old American. Miller did not consider himself a real writer, that is, one who writes with a purpose. Writing was like breathing to him. To Seferis he may have looked like a Louis Lambert, who had seen and come to terms with the "white angels," who had ceased looking for the miracle in "distant things" (to recall Seferis' epigraph from Pindar (to the *Erotikos Logos*, in *Collected Poems*: 479)), who had rather invented or created the miracle.

Seferis also knew that Miller's style of life was not necessarily his own style. He could not copy the man who had described himself as "chancre the crab, which moves sideways and backwards and forwards at will" (*Black Spring*: 1963: 29). In "Les anges sont blancs" and in *Meres C*, Seferis recorded Miller's message; he did not espouse it as a *modus vivendi* for himself. The American became in his mind an alternative, a different potentiality, a brilliant jester who never let the boredom of life overwhelm him, a half-conscious carrier of the miracle. From his side, Miller had perceived, as we noted earlier, in *The Colossus of Maroussi*, the special qualities of Seferis' mind and seemed eager to maintain their relationship. Miller wrote many more letters to Seferis than vice versa, and was the one who breathed fresh air into their correspondence when it slackened. In asking for a copy of *First Impressions of Greece* after Seferis' death, Miller acted in a sense as if he wanted their relationship to survive death or complete its full cycle.

Apart from the use of material derived from Miller in the poem, "Les anges sont blancs," it is difficult to say what else Seferis borrowed, consciously or unconsciously, from Miller in the rest of his poetry. After all, he was careful to assimilate or disguise whatever he borrowed from others[8] except from Eliot, where many of the loans (poetic motifs and critical ideas) are visible enough for us to identify.

In a letter that Seferis wrote to George Theotokas about Cyprus, on December 25, 1954, he expressed disappointment with the narrow colonial policy of Britain on the island. He also he had recourse to Miller's *The Colossus of Maroussi* (136): "You feel like shouting with him [that is, Miller] 'je m'en fous de la civilization européene.'" (Seferis-Theotokas: 158)— Miller had said this in a very different context, during his Cretan journey in 1939, to a Cretan's French wife who had expressed dissatisfaction with her life on the "savage" island, away from "civilization." One could also compare two entries from Seferis' diary, one from *Meres C* and the other from *Meres D*. The second, where Seferis speaks:

> This evening I read [Aeschylus'] *Septem* to the end; above all, the end. This poem makes you calm, gives you a great comfort. You know that neither the Italians nor the Bulgarians nor the Germans can take it from you or destroy it. Even if you feel you are ephemeral, you know that this work is not, you know that whatever of you is in there is not ephemeral,
> (*Meres D*: 33)

echoes Miller's words, confided to his Greek friends, just before he left Greece in 1939: "Nobody can now enslave me. What can they take from me? Beethoven's *Quartets*? The ideas which I love?— No." (*Meres C*: 152).

Miller may also have had something to do with Seferis' reaction to "flying," as it is recorded in (*Meres E*: 19). "In the air going to England. I think of Odysseus who struggled for ten years to return from Troy to Ithaki and find unpalatable the downhill path we have taken. We keep reducing earth, until it will turn into a hazel-nut. At the end we will inevitably throw it into the infinite void. The atomic bomb is a logical consequence, etc. etc." It is worth comparing this with Miller's peculiar reaction to his first flight, from Athens to Crete, in 1939— in fact, the flight had been arranged by Seferis who had decided, as Miller said, that he should ride in pomp: "I had never been in a plane before and I probably will never go up again. I felt foolish sitting in the sky with my hands folded... Man is made to walk the earth and sail the seas: the conquest of the air is reserved for a later stage of his evolution, when he will have sprouted real wings and assumed the form of the angel which he is in essence. Mechanical devices have nothing to do with man's real nature— they are merely traps which Death has baited for him." (*The Colossus of Maroussi*: 112-113). Seferis' reaction to his own first flight on an airplane, in 1928, was less critical, more impressionistic (*Meres A*: 104-105).

The juxtaposition of select passages from the work of Miller and that of Seferis suggests that there was a perhaps unconscious dialogue between the two men beside their intermittent correspondence. As *Meres D* shows, Miller was particularly in Seferis' mind during the days of the Second World War. We have seen Seferis thinking of writing to Miller on the ship that took him back to Greece from Italy in 1944. But we also have entries of 1942, one of January 10, 1942 (*Meres D*: 176), when Seferis, feeling sluggish, thought enviously of Miller "who strikes his typewriter like a pianist that has gone berserk"; or the second of January 21, 1942, when Seferis received *The Colossus of Maroussi* and translated it, orally, to his wife, skipping the pages which he had received previously in manuscript; or the third, of March 8, 1944, when he commented on a letter from Miller, the one in which he was advised to "explore Timbuctoo." (*Meres D*: 192). Again Miller was in Seferis' thoughts on the morning of Good Friday, 1942, as "a representative American of the great despair of the mid-war period" (*Meres D*: 206).

The saying "opposites attract each other" describes the relationship between Seferis and Miller, but it also implies that there was some deeper similarity, a common element that worked as a bond between them. That was the "inside out" quality that Miller had already claimed for himself when he found it in the poems of Seferis. The perception of reversal informs not only many of Seferis' poems (e.g. "Denial" of *Turning Point*, and the epigraph to this same collection, from the 17th century poem *Erotokritos*: "But everything went wrong for me and upside down,/ the nature of things was reborn for me") but also an earlier work, the "novel" *Six Nights on the Acropolis*, which Seferis first wrote in the late 1920s, reworked in the early 1950s, and left in a more or less publishable form. There are three passages in that work that are specially significant. In the first, Seferis describes a friend of his named Nicholas:

> His relationship with literature reminds you of an engineer who unscrews a machine and screws it back *inside out*. He has such a way of changing the analogies that he can turn the most tender or respectable things into monstrous or give to the most monstrous a coloration of mercy; this is his kind of humor. You'd say that he observes the world from a spot unknown to all of us. (17)

The second passage offers us an original view of springtime: "Spring, you'd say, works in reverse, not from below upwards but from above downwards; it pulls you inside the soil." (Ibid.: 74). In the more extensive third passage, Stratis (who is to be identified with Seferis) unveils his innermost feelings to his lover Bilio:

> [As a younger man] I tried to bare my heart as much as I could; go deeper, much deeper. At the end I found only a surface, flat and smooth, free of any extremities where the eye could take a hold: the absolute void and a frightening clarity of mind. You feel and see your senses fall and vanish in there like the drops of water at the end of a string. They call you and you do not know whom they call, him who looks at or him at whom he looks. Your smallest action ends up assuming the importance of a mortal combat. Do you know who Narcissus was? A man who saw himself drowning without being able to move and save himself... Then, I started escaping from that torment, little by little, persistently, dragging myself. I was trying to hold on to any object of the external world, an object whatsoever, however

insignificant. I needed to cut myself free from the terrible *inside*, like a baby. (Ibid.: 227-228)

What Seferis described above is of course the process by which he effected the reversal of view, or orientation, that was necessary for him to live and create. In this process, he was eventually helped by a man like Miller who had reached a similar kind of impasse in his life and cut through it like an Alexander cutting through the knot he could not untie. A hubris one might say. Yes, but a necessary one.

NOTES

1. Not incorrectly, perhaps, in a technical sense, but the term is wrong to the extent that it has been abusively applied by Greek critics to difficult poets like Seferis. Yet, Seferis did not practice surrealism, i.e., automatic writing, and thought of it as a superficial language.

2. Another instance, where a Seferis metaphor has been interpreted too metaphysically by critics is the opening of his *Three Secret Poems*: "Leaves like rusty tin/ for the desolate mind that has seen the end—/ the barest glimmerings./ Leaves aswirl with gulls/ made wild with winter." (*Collected Poems*: 399). In "leaves like rusty tin," Seferis may not have alluded to anything metaphysical but merely to the color that fallen leaves take on in autumn.

3. "Three 'Moments' with Seferis" [in Greek], *Diavazo*, 142 (April 23, 1986), 92-93.

4. We have a parallel in *Thrush*, III (*Collected Poems*: 337), where the serene image of carefree boys diving from the bowsprits of boats evoked for the poet images of "naked bodies plunging into black light/ with a coin between the teeth..."

5. I am grateful to Dr. E.S. Phinney for helping me transcribe Miller's manuscript.

6. The neo-classical "Iliou Melathron" (Palace of Ilion, or Troy) on Panepistimiou Street, in Athens, which Schliemann had built to be his official residence, passed, eventually, into the possession of the Greek State and served for many years as the headquarters of the Greek Supreme Court. More recently, it has been restored and used for exhibitions and cultural functions.

7. The Greek version, "Tris Meres sta Petrokomena Monastiria tis Kapadokias" (Three days in the stone-cut monasteries of Cappadocia) is now in *Dokimes*, II: 57-93.

8. Cf. Seferis' original note on *Thrush*, III: "And if you condemn me to drink poison, I thank you": "They asked me whether I had in mind 'King Lear's' verse: *if you have poison for me, I will drink it*. No; if I had thought of the verse, I would have changed my text." "They" must refer to Romilly Jenkins. See Chapter One, p. 24.

Bibliography

1. PRIMARY SOURCES

Seferis, George. 1948. *The King of Asine and Other Poems*. Trans. B. Spencer, N. Valaoritis, L. Durrell. Introduction by R. Warner. London: J. Lehmann.

———— 1960. *Poems*. Trans. R. Warner. London: Little Brown.

———— 1966. *On the Greek Style. Selected Essays in Poetry and Hellenism.* Trans. R. Warner and Th. Frangopoulos. Boston: Little Brown.

———— 1974. *Dokimes* [Essays]. Volumes I and II. Third Edition. Athens: Ikaros.

———— 1976. *Tetradio Yimnasmaton, B.* [Book of exercises, B]. Poems. Athens: Ikaros.

———— 1981. *Collected Poems*. Trans. E. Keeley and Ph. Sherrard. Expanded Edition. Princeton: Princeton University Press.

———— 1974. *Exi Nihtes stin Akropoli* [Six nights on the Acropolis]. Athens: Ermis.

———— 1965. *Andigrafes* [Copyings]. Translations from English and French Poetry. Athens: Ikaros.

———— 1975. *Seferis ke Theotokas.* Allilografia [Seferis and Theotokas. Correspondence]. Athens: Ermis.

———— 1985. *Seferis ke Diamantis.* Allilografia [Seferis and Diamantis. Correspondence]. Athens: Ermis.

———— 1975. *Meres A* [Days A]. February 16, 1925-August 17, 1931. Athens: Ikaros.

———— 1975. *Meres B* [Days B]. August 24, 1931-February 12, 1934. Athens: Ikaros.

———— 1977. *Meres C* [Days C]. April 16, 1934-December 14, 1940. Athens: Ikaros.

———— 1977. *Meres D* [Days D]. January 1, 1941-December 31, 1944. Athens: Ikaros.

———— 1973 *Meres E* [Days E]. January 1, 1945-April 19, 1951. Athens: Ikaros.

_____ 1986. *Meres F* [Days F]. April 20, 1951-August 4, 1956. Athens: Ikaros.

Durrell, Lawrence. 1985. *Collected Poems. 1931-1974*. London: Faber and Faber.

_____ 1962. *Prospero's Cell. A Guide to the Landscape and Manners of the Island of Corfu*. London: Faber and Faber.

_____ 1975. *Blue Thirst*. Santa Barbara: Capra Press.

_____ 1980. *The Greek Islands*. Penguin.

_____ 1969. *Spirit of Place. Letters and Essays on Travel*. Edited by A.G. Thomas. London: Faber and Faber.

Miller, Henry. 1941. *The Colossus of Maroussi*. New York: New Directions.

_____ 1963. *Black Spring*. New York: Grove Press.

_____ 1973. *First Impressions of Greece*. Santa Barbara: Capra Press.

2. SECONDARY SOURCES

Beaton, Roderick. 1976. "Life at Close Range" [Review of Seferis, *Meres B*]. *Times Literary Supplement*. September 17.

Capri-Karka, Carmen. 1985. *War in the Poetry of George Seferis*. New York: Pella.

Fermor, P.L. 1977. "The Art of Nonsense" [Review of Seferis, *Piimata me Zografies se Mikra Pedia* (Poems with drawings for small children). *Times Literary Supplement*. January 26.

Frazer, G.S. 1970. *Lawrence Durrell*. London: Longman Group Ltd.

Hadas, Rachel. 1985. *Form, Cycle, Infinity. Landscape Imagery in the Poetry of Robert Frost and George Seferis*. Lewisburg, PA: Bucknell University Press.

Keeley, Edmund. 1983. *Modern Greek Poetry. Voice and Myth*. Princeton University Press.

Kohler, Denis. 1985. *L'Aviron D'Ulysse. L'itinéraire poétique de Georges Seferis*. Paris: Société d' Édition "Les Belles Lettres."

Maronitis, D. 1984. *I Piissi tou Yorgou Seferi* [The poetry of George Seferis]. Athens: Ermis.

McCarthy, Eugene. 1985 "Reflections on George Seferis." *Modern Greek Studies Yearbook*, 1: 145-151.

Nakas, Th. 1978. *Parallila Horia sta Dokimia tou Seferi ke tou Eliot* [Parallel passages in the essays of Seferis and those of Eliot]. Athens: Private publication.

Rexine, J.E. 1987. "The Diaries of George Seferis as a Revelation of his Art." *World Literature Today*, (Spring): 220-223.

_____ 1987. "The Poetic and Political Conscience of George Seferis." *Modern Greek Studies Yearbook*, 3: 311-320.

Savidis, G., Ed. 1961: *Ya ton Seferi. Timitiko Afieroma sta Trianta Hronia tis Strophis* [For Seferis. A Festschrift on the thirtieth anniversary of *Turning Point*]. Athens: O Tahidromos.

Sherrard, Ph. 1972. "The Death of a Poet." *The London Magazine*, 12, 4: 6-22.

Spender, St. 1955. *Collected Poems. 1928-1953*. London: Faber and Faber.

Stanford, W.B. 1954. *The Ulysses Theme: a Study in the Adaptability of a Traditional Hero*. Oxford: Oxford University Press.

Stravinsky, I. 1970. *Poetics of Music*. With a preface by G. Seferis. Cambridge, MA: Harvard University Press.

Thaniel, G. 1983. *Homage to Byzantium. The Life and Work of Nikos Gabriel Pentzikis*. Minneapolis: North Central Publishing Company.

Tsatsos, I. 1982. *My Brother George Seferis*. Trans. J. Demos. Minneapolis: North Central Publishing Company.

Vayenas, N. 1979. *O Piitis ke O Horeftis* [The poet and the dancer]. Athens: Kedros.

Young, K. 1950. "The Contemporary Greek Influence on English Writers." *Life and Letters*, 64: 53-64.

Special Issues of Journals: 1972. *Alif*, 2 (June); 1979. *The Coffeehouse*, 9; 1985. *I Lexi* [The word], 43; 1979 and 1983. *Labrys*, 5 and 8.

ABOUT THE AUTHOR

GEORGE THANIEL was born in Trahila, Messinia, Greece, in 1938, and died in Athens in 1991. He received his B.A. degree from the University of Athens in 1962. He emigrated to Canada in 1964, where he received his Ph.D. degree from MacMaster University, Hamilton, in 1971. He taught modern Greek studies at the University of Toronto from 1972 until his death in June 1991.

George Thaniel was a lyric poet and literary critic in Greek and English. His most significant book of poems was *The Nails* (1968; 1981 second edition), and his most important books of literary criticism were *The Lepidopterist of Suffering, Nikos Kachtitsis* (1981) and *Homage to Byzantium: The Life and Work of Nikos Gabriel Pentzikis* (1983). He was a member of the Classical Association of Canada, the American Philological Association, and the Modern Greek Studies Association of America.

ABOUT GEORGE SEFERIS

GEORGE SEFERIS won the Nobel Prize for Literature in 1963; he was a lyric poet of international standing. His major works of poetry included *Mythistorima* ("Novel," 1935), *Logbooks I-III* (1940, 1945, & 1955), *Cyprus, where it was Decreed* (1955), and *Three Secret Poems* (1966). The most important volume of his collected poetry was *Poems, 1924-46*. He received an honorary doctorate degree from Cambridge University in 1960, and later honorary doctorates from Oxford, Thessaloniki, and Princeton. He was an Honorary Fellow of the American Academy of Arts and Sciences.

Seferis was born in Smyrna, Asia Minor, in 1900, and died in Athens in 1971. He was educated in Athens and Paris. He made his career in the Greek diplomatic service, and in 1941 he followed the Greek government into exile, returning to Athens in 1944. The friendships with English-speaking friends that are memorialized in this book grew up in 1931-34 when he was acting Consul General in London; in 1944, when he flew from Egypt to England carrying messages from the exiled Greek government; in 1951-52 when he was First Counsellor in London; and in 1957-62 when he was Ambassador of Greece to England.